Albatross

Albatross

John A. Wills

Writers Club Press
San Jose New York Lincoln Shanghai

Albatross

Writers Club Press
an imprint of iUniverse.com, Inc.

For information address:
iUniverse.com, Inc.
5220 S 16th, Ste. 200
Lincoln, NE 68512
www.iuniverse.com

ISBN: 0-595-19418-4

Printed in the United States of America

DEDICATED

to the staff of Stourbridge Library,
where much of this book was written.

CONTENTS

L'ALBATROS

Souvent, pour s'amuser, les hommes d'équipage
Prennent des albatros, vastes oiseaux des mers,
Qui suivent, indolents compagnons du voyage,
La navire glissant sur les gouffres amers.

Apeine les ont-ils deposés sur les planches,
Que ces rois de l'azur, maladroits et honteux,
Laissent piteusement leurs grandes aîles blanches
Comme des avirons trainer a coté d'eux.

Ce voyageur ailé, comme il est gauche et veule!
Lui naguère si beau, qu'il est comique et laid!
L'un agace son bec avec un brûle-gueule,
L'autre mime, en boîtant, l'infirme qui volait!

Le Poète est semblable au prince des nuées,
Qui hante la tempête et se rit de l'archer;
Exilé sur le sol au milieu des huées,
Ses aîles de géant l'empêchent de marcher.

Baudelaire: Spleen et Idéal II
The Albatross

Sometimes, to raise a laugh, the seamen in a crew
Capture albatrosses, vast fliers of the seas,
Those idle tag-alongs, who shadow o'er the blue
The ships that slide upon the bitter waves and breeze.

Once they have put them down upon the ship's broad deck
These kings of azure sky clumsy and shameful flop;
Their mighty snow-white wings go dragging in a wreck,
Like helpless rowing oars that neither start nor stop.

This traveller on wings, oh how he's gauche and weak!
Just shortly proud in flight, now laughed at, low must must

sigh!

One sailor with a pipe bangs at the silly beak,
Another, limping, mocks the cripple who could fly!

The Poet is the same as that prince of the clouds
Who haunts the tempest dark and laughs at hunter's bow;
Exiled upon the ground, amidst the woeful crowds,
His giant wings impede all progress he should know.

John A. Wills   1993.09.27

Wisdom

MERTON VS RAND

Not long ago in a thrift shop I found Thomas Merton: *Disputed Questions*. This book, says the blurb, shows clearly that the big thing wrong with modern society is too much individualism. A shelf below was Ayn Rand: *For the New Intellectual*. This, says *its* blurb, attacks the atmosphere of guilt, of panic, of despair, of boredom and of all-pervasive evasion created by the prevalent doctrines of altruism and collectivism.

I have read neither of these books, but I have read other works by the same authors. I am sure that if, being neither a bigot nor a fool, you read either of these books with your brain switched on you will agree with 80% of it. That will still be true after you have read both of them. But they cannot both be right—Rand and Merton were contemporaries and both lived in the United States. Furthermore, both were knowledgeable and intelligent—hence your agreement with both of them—so they are not likely both to be wrong; indeed, it is unlikely that you will find a major error in either at plain reading(you will probably find some minor errors of fact and perhaps of logic, but nothing to pull either book apart).

The usual response of the wishywashy to this kind of impasse is to say evasively(one thing Rand definitely had right!) that there is something right with both sides(without saying just what) and the truth lies somewhere in the middle(If I want to live in Amblecote, and my wife in Bedcote, we should buy a narrow-boat and moor it under the Stour Bridge). Another not uncommon response is to take sides by religion and personal morality: I might prefer Merton's view because he was an ascetic Christian whereas Rand was an adulterous atheist. But this does not wash: Merton would be as emphatic as Rand despite her own life in preaching that "morality is not a contest of whims"; more, despite his personal holiness, Merton was obviously

3

not informed by God that certain people were leading him up the garden path about the Vietnam War. I am sure that personal morality is a help to the right answers, but it is obviously not enough, nor, depending on the kind of argument, is it necessary. We have to look at the arguments; play the board, not the man.

We cannot in reason judge on the basis of our comfort in reading either author, quite apart from the fact that different people will feel differently gritty with the two authors: it may be precisely the truth that we find uncomfortable, either from habits of thought(It took me years to reconcile myself to the floating-continent theory) or from self-recognition("You are the man", as Nathan said to David). We must, to use Rand's terminology, refer to demonstrable principles.

This kind of disagreement is common in both politics and religion. Part of the problem is in the differing assumptions people make about the world, part in the various ambiguities of words and phrases and even underlying concepts. We can read either Rand or Merton to absorb a rich world view of the doctrine of each; we can read both, each time ignoring the reflexes induced by the other. Except for minor matters we are not likely to find falsity in either.

Well, we know what that means, don't we children? There is a category error lurking somewhere. The individualism/collectivism dichotomy looks a good candidate for a first investigation—but I would have to read both books carefully, get into the mood of each of them, before being at all sure. Distinction of detachment and selfishness may also help(Orwell has a relevant remark). One central category error found, secondary ones will emerge, and probably a lot of identity errors too. Getting both books straight, and integrating them into a harmonious whole(for both undoubtedly contain much of value), will be a long hard slog. Ingrained habits of mind will have to be replaced, for no doubt the detection of Merton's and Rand's errors will involve detection of the detector's too. Has anyone the honesty, courage and patience for the task? Has anyone the time and library resources for it(we need the library for dictionaries and for related reading to tease out the concepts at issue), the word processing facilities? Actually, most professional philosophers nowadays probably have the library and word processing facilities, but honesty, courage and patience are something else.

A similar problem to the above arises in comparative religion. One would think that this discipline would consist of comparisons of the answers given by various religions to the various questions we call "religious", but in practice that is not how it looks. For each religion we start from scratch, and simple comparison is something exceptional, and often not actually religious(knowing about the difference between morning Buddha Hall and Terce is not knowing about the difference between Buddhism and Christianity). We do not compare the different answers of the various religions at least in part because they are not answering the same questions. The first question to which to give comparative answers should perhaps be "What are the questions each religion tries to answer?", and the next "Which questions does each religion think important?". To this there seems at present no systematic answer, probably for the same reason as we find no answer to the Rand/Merton dichotomy: lurking conceptual errors.

In 1900 David Hilbert proposed at Paris his famous list of 23 problems for 20th-century mathematicians to solve(or show to be insoluble). Most of the work has now been completed. I think we need a similar program for the philosophers of the 21st century. There may also be a need for a list for the psychologists, including the problem of showing people the importance of the philosophical problems. But we are honest people here, are we not? We know that the shift from mediaeval to Daltonian chemistry was largely a distinction of categories; we can see that questions like the Levant, gayness and others are fairly easily solved once certain errors of thought are recognized; we know this technique set of conceptual(often called "linguistic") analysis, Hume's "accurate and abstract philosophy", as the great achievement of 20th-century philosophers, and we recognize the stubborn shyness of many of those professional philosophers willing to tackle Hume's "easy and humane philosophy"(which is clearly *not* easy) to look through the logico-metaphysical glasses so assiduously polished by the scholastics and the analysts.

Matters such as the Levant and gayness can be considered as riders or exercises preparatory to the imposing problems of social philosophy I started this essay by considering, and the colossal problems of religion exemplified by the lack of system in the discipline of comparative religion. Those who fear results different from ones already espoused will complain of essentialism and slavery to words. Those who want quick answers(preferably requiring no great rearrangement of their own ideas), or are satisfied with the cleverness fairly simple analysis lets them display, will refuse to take the time to understand the opposing doctrines of those such as Rand and Merton; they may claim such work to be as useless as the thorough study of Heidegger or Derrida probably is. But the right Paris Program for the 21st Century would bring a greater expansion of human understanding(not just knowledge) than that in any earlier century.

Let us think of some problems.

1. Merge all that is valuable of Rand's and Merton's social theory into a coherent whole.

2. Specify the questions on the basis of the answers to which may be asked the questions the various religions attempt to answer, and list the basis answers in common terminology, relating that common terminology to the terminology actually used in the various religions. Then ask in common terminology the questions the religions attempt to answer, indicating the answers that the various religions propose, correlating so far as the nature of the questions allows the various lower-level answers among the religions.

3. Find commonality of definition of such concepts as human dignity, human rights, state of nature and government, democracy and the socialist/liberal and other political (dis)continua, to construct a question set within which political opinions can be consistently compared.

4. We all know what consciousness is, but we cannot easily define it. This must be because we do *not* know what we mean by it. Analyse extant literature to distinguish and relate the various meanings. The literature analysed must include at least Jaynes: *Origin of Consciousness* and Chalmers: *Conscious Mind.*

5. Define Philosophy, noting that at least three distinguishable disciplines(weltanschauung description, mathesis universalis(accurate and abstract), ethics(easy and humane)) are at present lumped together.

1996.02.23

Coda: since writing the above, I have read both of the books which inspired it. The blurb for the Merton was very misleading, but I think my conclusion from it is still valid.

1997.05.10

SERPENT GROUP

In 1969 Bertrand Russell experienced the Particular Judgement. Warned, he was armed with an answer to the question "Why didn't you believe in me?". I think the most likely first question was "Why did you support Hitler against the Poles and Ho against the South Vietnamese?". Perhaps I am wrong.

But Bruce Kent seems to agree with me that our political activity is more important to God than theological details: "The more Christians work as partners in the building of the Kingdom, the easier Christian unity is going to be."(Universe 1995.02.19 p.14). What an image he evokes:

Oh beautiful for patriot dream
that sees beyond the years
Thine alabaster cities gleam
undimmed by human tears.

(Katherine L. Bates)

The last time I sang that I went out into a city with alabaster(let's not be literalists) enough but much dimmed with human tears. There is much to do.

But Bruce Kent is himself rather a pacifist than a builder of the Kingdom, and with communitarian tendencies too, seeking a society rather like that of Swift's Houyhnhnms, in which, as Orwell pointed out, the arbiter of behaviour is public opinion, less tolerant than any system of law. When a pacifist calls "peace!" he is more often than not promoting some particularly nasty tyrant:

Mark where his carnage and his conquests cease
He makes a wilderness and calls it peace.

(Byron)

Let us look at some other Christians organized as such for the political building of the Kingdom. Christian Aid has recently been lambasting the IMF and its subsidiaries for Structural Adjustment Programs, which have, we are told, been impoverishing Third-World people. I was invited to the Birmingham teach-in on this subject and got propaganda in advance. By careful reading I decided that Christian Aid was complaining about people getting cheaper food, to the chagrin of formerly monopolistic suppliers—various equivalents of Europe's rape and banana growers. With a little special knowledge I was able to deduce that some of the ills portrayed resulted from heavy militarization, which the IMF never demands. Of course, this kind of lambasting of the big guys is dramatic and provides a quick emotional release, but allying ourselves with comparatively well-off people afraid of competition and others more eager to build certain kinds of anarchic community than to empower families and individuals to choose among sources of food and other goods is most emphatically **not** the way to help the poor.

The same Christian Aid pack had some worship suggestions. We are supposed to kid ourselves that Dt 24:19 commands the state to pay subsidies to the producers of staple foods, although, as simply reading it will tell you, the verse forbids farmers to harvest thoroughly, so that the poor will be able to glean; this is a very appropriate rule for farmers where there is rural poverty, but who are Christian Aid's partners? Dt 23:19, which seems to have direct relevance, condemning as it does loans at interest, might appropriately have been used to condemn the World Bank(one of the IMF's subsidiaries), but was not, because the alternative, equity investment, implies greater freedom than Christian Aid's partners are willing to countenance. It also implies, of course, that our own retirement savings should go into PEPs rather than TESSAs—far too near the bone!

Not long ago another allegedly Christian-inspired peace group spoke in our Parish Hall about El Salvador. I used to read a daily paper also read by many Central Americans, so I had some knowledge about the place in the back of my mind, and before the talk I refreshed my memories by looking things up in *Britannica* yearbooks. I asked about a very important point of the law of El Salvador: had civil immunity of government officers been abolished? Three times I asked this question; three times it was clumsily dodged. Yet this may be at the heart of the ills afflicting El Salvador, so presumably the speaker knew the answer but found it irrelevant to the plans supported for El Salvador. Perhaps his friends intended to shelter under the same immoral umbrella on coming to power(which they didn't in the subsequent election).

Many allegedly Christian Kingdom-builders have the unanalytic mind incapable of recognizing its own handiwork. In the case of Russell(who did not, of course, call himself a Christian) this failure of analysis is quite extraordinary.

To build the Kingdom we need discipline, commitment and responsibility. The last includes the patience, honesty and courage to go back and relearn what we thought we already knew when we find something wrong in our ideas. Will this, like Oscar Wilde's socialism, take too many evenings? Probably; that explains why we are not doing it. We with the honesty and intelligence to plot the way to the Kingdom have been as gentle as doves too long, and now should wake up and become as cunning as serpents. We should form **Serpent Groups** of intelligent individuals willing to separate concerns.

In his last interview, Anthony Burgess was asked by Elvira Huelbos of the Madrid *Mundo*: "Are you grateful for being Catholic?"; he answered: "It has taught me to think logically". The Serpent Group is not then for rhetoric but for logic, not for intuition but for consciousness. There we recognize that there are political questions prior to left-versus-right, devolution-versus-subsidiarity, particular political boundaries, church-state relations, etc. In the 1960s it became customary for political speakers to preface ideological principles, conditional predictions, unlikely conjectures, woolly suppositions and downright lies with an emphatic "*FACT*". That must not be our way.

The first separation of concerns is that of ideal from strategy and of both from tactics. The next is of different levels of political discourse. We might, like the speaker on El Salvador, be disappointed in the results of democracy for which we have worked, or at least spoken, but we should have the honesty to recognize that who should have power is distinct from how power should be used, not complain at a lack of "true" or "real" or "participatory" democracy. I remember a Marxist extolling a dictatorship for its health service(not, I think, as good as he claimed) and calling a health service a more important part of democracy than elections(which the country hadn't had for over 30 years)—but it is not a part of democracy at all. When I was 11 I read a book claiming that for democracy state ownership of the means of production was essential—but even an 11-year-old can and should see that a democracy might choose other modes of economy. Those in a Serpent Group must make such distinctions reflexively, and be willing to train themselves in further distinctions (Christianity gives not comfort but endless potential) as appropriate.

A Christian friend of mine shies at such approaches to problems, quoting *Tao Te Ching* 1:2—míng ke míng fëi cháng míng-, which he translates "It's not all words, John". I am glad he is not victim to the famous Buddhistized interpretations, but he should realize that the ideal of peasant life is not such as a Christian should embrace and the previous verse— dào ke dào fëi cháng dào, i.e. we have no idea of the road we're on—is flat contrary to Jesus's claim to be the Way(Jn 14:6).

Suppose we form a Serpent Group in our parish(obviously we would happily have members from other Christian denominations). If we can keep honest, acknowledging even uncomfortable facts, we should be able to formulate ideals. Perhaps Churches Together would leave the chairmanship of the hustings to us, or let us formulate the first questions. We could construct a theoretical manifesto, ever ready to revise it, strictly topdown structured(and so quite likely to be consistent), and hang from it a set of strategies; One of us might bring an essay for the rest of us to find flaws in; other modes of debate are possible. Our tactics for implementation would perhaps be very individual.

I am not volunteering to organize a Serpent Group. It should meet in the house of someone with a fairly good library—I do not expect all the blue-bound volumes of *Statutes in Force*, but at least half the time when we need to look at an important text it should be available—and a PC taking either size of diskette, for sharing essays and the like. The participants should have some knowledge of social and political structures, and recognize the inter-relatedness of issues. They should be able not only to separate but to relate concerns. The chairman should have enough knowledge of psychology to know when to shut me(oh yes, I'll join, I just won't host or organize it) up for waffling and when to allow me to expound a necessary background for an idea I want to submit.

If a Serpent Group gets started, someone please tell me. Or is it too much like work to meet thus one evening a month and a few extra times in the run-up to elections? Is it too many evenings?

1995.02.24

LOOKING AT UNEMPLOYMENT

Soon I will complete 5 years of unemployment. I have experienced the difficulty of finding work, despite quite a lot of government help(Job clubs for half of each year; fare to interview; and so forth), then sadness of using savings for storage costs and daily living(what savings are for, but not what I had planned). An inappropriate environment has re-induced an old bad dream the NHS seems quite incompetent at killing.

In the background, certain God-imposed obligations become more intractable, but I can do nothing about them without a firmer material and psychological basis. Other things which I cannot do unless I have an income also become more difficult the more I delay. You might expect some kinds of bitterness at my frustration. But what good is bitterness?

God is working in the world and, as Macchiavelli wrote, is not willing to do everything and thus take away our free will and our share of glory. I see His plans stumble forward, hindered by sin, and choose not to add to that sin. I try to work for my share of glory: obviously, heavy job seeking(I am notorious among government agencies for maximum use of facilities), with some emphasis on places good for the other tasks I know God has given me, appropriate self-improvement(HMG has interesting training courses), local value to others(teaching adult illiterates to read, minor research for local LIFE group),… lots to do.

The recruiting pamphlet for the RAChD has the stories of several chaplains; one ends his tale "I'm sure I'm where God wants me to be". I am in one sense where God wants me, because I got here by my considered actions, taking God's apparent wishes into account, in the context of forces outside my control. But I am where God does not want me, in the sense that he wants me to try might and main to change my status, whereas that chaplain has no command from the Lord to seek a new position. God wants me to be where I am, i.e. trying to be somewhere else.

I suffer that variant of "over-qualification" sometimes known as "golden handcuffs". I am not in quite the same boat as most of the unemployed. They hinder my re-employment because they are my rivals and because they are not buying the goods and services which I might provide. So I am interested in the general pattern of unemployment from a self-interested as well as a quasiscientific point of view.

The first thing I notice is that unemployment in the North is counterbalanced by an easier situation in the South, due in large part to fairer trade. I am not a rival of many Third-World people, but my potential clients sometimes are. I am a victim of the world becoming a better place.

The second is like to the first: when Eastern Electricity, producing the same amount of electricity, fired half its staff(something the other electricity companies are about to copy), idiots like Paul Foot blamed privatization for increasing unemployment, but a conscientious administration of a state-owned industry would never have let a quarter of the staff in effect cancel the work of another quarter. Restructuring causes unemployment because the previous structure was misusing people's effort and skills. These will eventually be re-engaged by those benefiting from the restructuring(the owners of a privatized industry, presumably the customers of a state-owned one), but the adjustment will take a while.

Another apparent cause of unemployment—*inter alia* of difficulty in moving house—is that we are going from high inflation to low. Last year's Nobel Economics prize was for a detailed analysis of the ways governments deceive employers into temporary over-employment to induce a feel-good factor in time for an election. But all who had ever bothered to think about the matter knew anyway that such stopgaps did more harm than good. Misunderstanding of Keynes is the justification for being fooled in this way. There is no serious doubt that the end of inflation is good for everyone except a few swindlers, not all of whom are politicians; like fairer trade, it lets us work better.

The above difficulties lead many people into two errors. The first is the theory the Venda call *zwivhuya*, that there is only a fixed amount of wealth available and that therefore anyone who has more than average is a thief: envy of the rich masquerades as concern for the poor. The other error is almost the opposite: the illusion of the one-sided coin, which allows politicians to neglect the weak and appease the powerful with tariffs and like practices.

Someone in the dole queue with me a few months ago was proposing the banning of automation. He had seen it coming—but not bothered to retrain himself either in the new techniques of his own trade or in some other trade. Nor had he made any attempt to broaden his general education(everyone should have at least 8 GCSEs) so as to maximize his adaptability. We see redundancy, but the other side of the automation coin is more product from less factor, surely desirable. We know that earlier automation has been followed by reductions in unemployment, because there is plenty of work to be done in the world. But some people claim a right of perpetual stagnation, which they justify via the one-sided-coin theory.

I am too honest to let myself be deceived by these, and I get annoyed when others—some through lack of education, some through sheer pigheadedness—take them up, sometimes both at once(envy of the rich coexists strangely with advocacy of unjust social stagnation).

No reasonable person wants any of these causes of unemployment abolished, and the protectionism which might temporarily save a few jobs in the North is a serious sin against the people of the South—not to mention consumers, who cannot unite as producers can.

I have, as you can see, a fairly rosy view of things. These changes blamed for evil are actually not very heavily disguised blessings. Watching the world improve in this way, I must try to maximize my own value and wealth(these words, Ruskin tells us, are related) within it.

I am not of those who expect the state to provide employment, nor of those who think consumption secondary to production, nor yet of those who refuse to retrain, or culpably keep themselves in ignorance. Further education cannot make golden handcuffs worse and may just help me re-slot myself into the world of work. So I have been doing a half load at the Open University, and a B.A. has now become a B.A.(Hons(1st)). If I ever resume my former career I will quite likely be better at it. I had to change lodgings to make the upgrade practicable. I hope I do not have to change again until in new employment.

I am starting a PGCE course, not because I want to be a teacher, although prior experience indicates I am suitable, but because the things I most want to do, am well able to do, and for which there seems to be a need, are things no-one wants to employ me to do.

I became unemployed at the same time as my house was sold and my household goods went into storage for the duration, expected to be less than three months(it took me a while to recognize the golden handcuffs). I was not eligible for income support until my house sale money was exhausted, so I will have no down payment for a new house. Also, housing benefit does not cover goods in storage. Obviously, as a matter of fairness among different classes of those down on their luck(those these benefits are for), the rules should change, and I have so told my MP. I may never benefit from such a change, but perhaps due to my suggestion others will experience greater fairness.

I have no fixed points, just pointers: family connections, formal academic work, the church everywhere, the things I know I must do once employed, patterns of reading, my approaches to my MP to tell him how to make the world better(he often listens), ever greater understanding of that world.

I am too intelligent to get angry at God for the big picture and my present place in it; I do get angry at hindrances to progress He allows, such as losing my briefcase this morning and my spectacle case this afternoon(No, I do not *blame* myself for every forgetfulness). Employed people have far more of the resources useful for the unemployed than the unemployed themselves have. But I am used enough to the idea of big pictures, the reverse sides of tapestries, and such-like, not to despair of rhyme or reason.

1996.02.21

Note: GCSE = General Certificate of Secondary Education,
a public examination normally sat at age 16 but open to and often sat by adults
HMG = Her Majesty's Government
LIFE = Life Is For Everyone, similar to the U.S.
Birthright
NHS = (UK) National Health Service
PGCE = Post-Graduate Certificate of Education
RAChD = Royal Army Chaplaincy Department

WHEN ATLAS SHRUGS

An Objectivist is thoroughly selfish. His own interests are the sole criterion of his morality. He cultivates self-esteem, the self-assurance of competence and adequacy, not self-respect, the habit of action by which we share with others the good that happens to us and retain to ourselves the bad. He may risk his life if he calculates with high probability that he will win something for himself, but he will not work without return either alone or jointly for the good of others of present or future generations, as an altruist might. Some altruists claim that a good intention justifies bad methods, and the Objectivist agrees with most altruists in condemning this doctrine, but the Objectivist condemns even the altruist who does no harm: sacrifice is gravely sinful. If he sees you drowning and does not know you, he will assume that you, like him, are rational(no rational, i.e. thoroughly selfish, person's interests conflict with another's), so may be of use to him some day, so he may throw you a lifebelt, but he will take no risks for your life.

There were once some virtuous, very selfish people who planned a better, selfish world, without all the altruism which was hurting them(e.g. by taxes for the good of others). Each of them thought himself likely to endure the time of trial and live thereafter in the new, virtuous, selfish world, so each thought the conspiracy worthwhile. Their leader was one John Galt, who so worked not because he loved them(what a horrible thought!) but because he would get something out of it for himself: "I will not live for any other man, nor ask any other man to live for me".

Selfish people do not strictly speaking love, but they experience something similar in admiration for the beautiful selfishness of another person, as they might love some piece of music. In this restricted sense, John and

Dagny were lovers. When the wicked altruists learnt of the conspiracy they decided to arrest John and extract from him the information needed to crush the good, selfish conspiracy. Anticipating this, John discussed with Dagny what to do if she too were arrested, for the altruists would torture her to persuade John to spill the beans, but then the conspiracy would end and he would never see the virtuous, selfish society he was so selfishly working for. But it would give him unbearable pain to see Dagny tortured, as it would give him pain to hear a beautiful piece of music 'murdered' by poor execution. So, if she were arrested, he would kill himself. He would not do this for the sake of the new world, for he had no interest in it except for himself. Neither would he kill himself to stop Dagny being tortured, for he had no interest in her when he could not experience or know about her. He carefully told her that his death would not be a sacrifice but purely selfish.

adapted from Ayn Rand: *Atlas Shrugged*

A martyr is a man who cares so much for something outside himself that he forgets his own personal life. A suicide is a man who cares so little for anything outside himself that he is willing to see the end of everything.

GKC: *Flag of the World*

A martyr has self-respect, a suicide self-esteem. Considering John Galt's motive for suicide, we see that the death of Dagny would have been almost as good as his own. When we have a sick dog put down, i.e. killed, we do so because the living music we saw in its life is being tortured and our appreciation of it turns to pain, not because we intellectually honestly think that death makes the dog better off. We transfer suicide from ourself to the dog. Most justifications of euthanasia are equally dishonest.

1995.07.19

Analysis

A CHANGE IN QUESTION

Up until the 17th Century, European scientists described matter and its transformations in terms of 4 elements: earth, water, air and fire. Because that did not explain all the reactions they observed, they postulated a fifth element, the quintessence.

By the beginning of the 19th Century, they believed in about 20 elements. One by one they added new elements to their list, Mendeleev organized the elements into a pattern so they knew what new elements to look for, and now there are about 100 known elements.

The change in the 18th Century was not just an adding of new elements to get from a list of 5 to a list of 20: none of the old 5 are to be found in the new 20! We might imagine chemists patiently finding out new things and gradually re-interpreting their old observations, which is how they got from 4 to 5 and, in a much longer process, from 20 to 100; but that is not how they got from 5 to 20. In the new scheme water is a compound, so you might imagine that a list of 5 substances had been expanded by finding that they were compounds rather than elements; but this would be true only of water and, at a stretch, air. Something much more radical was happening.

The old 5 elements were not in the same category as the new 20. Not only were the scientists of the 18th Century redescribing the world in terms of 20 elements; they were redescribing it in terms of 3 states of matter: solid, liquid, gas. The earlier scientists had not made this distinction very clearly, but obviously they wanted to describe phenomena which we now describe in terms of the 3 states. And indeed the old 4 elements correspond a little better to the new 3 states than to the new 20 elements:

earth to solid, water to liquid, air to gas(almost, fire to plasma). We cannot sensibly make any such parallel to the new substance elements.

As the substance elements can be combined to form further substances, compounds, so the states of matter can be combined to form colloids. Under the old system scientists had been struggling to describe the world in terms of combinations of the old elements, but after the great transformation of chemistry they were able to describe it in two distinct sets of terms.

In the 18th Century scientists were asking about both state and substance, instead of about one category as before, but they did not quite realize it, so that there were frequent messy echoes of the old system. Becher and Stahl, for instance, proposed that there was an element, which they named phlogiston, rather like the old fire element. Lavoisier and company said that Becher and Stahl were wrong as to fact, but really they were confusing questions: there is actually a *third* question involved here: whether matter or energy is involved. The state, substance and matter/energy problems are all intertwined, but they must be asked distinctly.

The old scientists were making a *category error*, i.e. they were answering several questions as if they were one question. The same happens when people think tabasco sauce is hot so you need gloves to carry a bottle of it. Another kind of word error is the *identity error*, in which, for instance, someone says "India", meaning the Indian Empire, and a moment later meaning the Republic of India, drawing conclusions about political rights and wrongs.

Category errors and identity errors are very common. One of the reasons we study language is precisely to enable us to recognize and avoid them. If you are discussing Northern Ireland it is a good idea to have in your mind a list of all the different meanings of the word *Britain*; if the Levant is your topic, the even messier use of the word *Israel*, where both category and identity errors crop up apace, is liable to invalidate your reasoning. Other category errors arise in use of the words *creation* and *homosexual*, by the former of which two quite complicated questions may be answered and by the latter three.

It is good practice to make lists of the definitions different people seem to have of various emotive words. You will then, no longer tripping over words, be better able to tackle the actual issues at stake in each discussion.

1995.10.27

CREATION

The answer *creation* has two meanings, depending on the question. Always be sure whether the word is being used as an answer in theology or in biology(perhaps extended to other natural sciences).

A. In Theology we notice that some things seem to be God and some seem to be Nature, or Matter(here including energy and whatever else physicists study). We ask ourselves what the relations are among God, Nature, reality and illusion. First we ask whether God is real, and two answers are possible.

    I. *Atheism* is the answer that there is no God; whatever seems to be God is some kind of illusion. If we accept this answer, we next inquire whether Nature is real. Two answers are possible.

        1. *Solipsism* is the answer that Nature, like God, is an illusion. Only I exist. Everything else is my imagination. Mark Twain may have been a Solipsist(cf. his book *Mysterious Stranger*).

        2. *Materialism* is the answer that Nature does exist. Anything which seems to be God is part of Nature which we mistake for God. This is the belief of orthodox Marxists, Objectivists and indeed most Atheists.

    II. The answer that God exists has, so far as I know, no general name. If we accept that God exists, we may next ask whether Nature exists. Two answers are possible.

        1. *Pan(en)theism* is the answer that there is no Nature, only God and perhaps some emanations of God:

whatever seems to be Nature is really God in some disguise. This belief, a mirror image of Materialism, is what some Hindus believe: Bhagavad-Gita 7:8-12.

2. *Distinctionism* is what I call the belief that God and Nature both really exist distinctly. If we accept this, we next inquire how God and Nature interact.

    a. *Dualism* is the answer that God and Matter exist independently. Those who believe—or seem to believe—this include the Albigensians or Catharists.

    b. *Creation* is the answer that Nature exists because God makes it. If we accept Creation, we may next ask what God does with Nature besides create it. I give two extreme answers.

        i. *Deism* is the answer 'not much'. It is what Freemasons traditionally believe: God is the Great Architect but does not care much what happens in his edifice.

        ii. *Theism* is the answer that God is interested in Nature at all levels. This is the theory given in Gn 1:1—2:4a.

Note: It is sometimes difficult to classify someone's response to the theological question. Theological answers are often used to describe not formal opinions but attitudes.

B. In *Biology* we notice that living things produce other living things like themselves, i.e. of the same species, in an at first sight endless chain. For each species so reproducing itself we can ask whether the chain of reproduction ever started, i.e. whether there was a beginning to the species. Obviously, two answers are possible.

I. *Permanence* is the answer that a species has always existed, never having begun: there always have been humans, or rabbits, or cuckoos. This seems to be the assumption of those who wrote the Buddhist *Jataka* tales(I do not say that it is a Buddhist teaching).

II. *Origination* is the answer that a species now reproducing itself started at some time in the past. If we decide that a particular species started at some time, the obvious next question is how. Two answers are imaginable.

    1. *Evolution* from a different species, not itself necessarily living, as proposed by people from Heracleitus to Darwin. This is the theory accepted by the majority of biologists for the vast majority of species. Hansen: *Animal Diversity* (Prentice-Hall) surveys the evidence for this theory and for the other imaginable answer.

    2. *Special Creation*, often called simply *Creation*, is the answer that a species arose outside ordinary chemical and biological activity, by some intervention. If we accept this, we may next ask what kind of intervention. There are three answers.

        a. Accident. For example, many biologists believe that prions, such as cause scrapie and BSE, result from accidents within mammalian cells.

        b. Spontaneity, i.e. something automatic in nature, e.g.:

            i. biologists formerly believed that maggots arose automatically within certain kinds of muck.

            ii. modern biologists believe that the wasp *Cotesia congregata* naturally creates polydnaviruses within itself.

c. Intention. Then…who intended it?

    i. Angels, to benefit humanity.

    ii. Devils, to hurt humanity.

    iii. Human scientists or technologists. Some people, for example, think that government scientists developed the AIDS virus. We can imagine this.

    iv. God, interrupting his work of Creation(in the theological sense). The noisiest who believe this are Fundamentalist Christians, who confuse Creation in the biological sense and Creation in the theological sense, like those who think that one needs gloves to carry Tabasco sauce because it is 'hot'.

    v. Intelligent species from another planet, for technical, artistic, idle or political reasons. Larry Niven in his *Known Space* series imagines an intelligent species creating a new species to fool a third species. This is an imaginable answer.

    vi. Further answers: exercise for the reader.

Note: It is rather unlikely that the Bible will help us in deciding how to answer the biological question, just as it is rather unlikely that Darwin's *Origin of Species* will help us with the theological question.

1995.07.14
rev. 1997.11.01

INTRODUCTION TO SEXUALITY

People talk a lot of rubbish about sexuality, and human eroticism in general. Sometimes they do this dishonestly, sometimes merely carelessly. The rubbish often derives from lack of firmness in use of names, so that much of it is nonsense or based on nonsensical assumptions. The aim of this essay is to review the relevant terminology in a systematic manner, not inventing new names(that is for scientific nomenclature conferences) but relating the various names available and pointing out some possible ambiguities. When we speak in a consistent manner about conjugation in general, we will be able to talk more sensibly about sexuality and in particular human eroticism. When our vocabulary is consistent and we describe nature truthfully with our vocabulary we will be better able to draw truthful and useful conclusions about psychological, social and moral issues.

We are sometimes warned not to be much influenced by essentialist reasoning, i.e. by linguistic analysis and biology, because human eroticism transcends mere biology. That may be true(I believe it is), but whatever we are we are on the basis of materiality and in particular of biology. There are numbers, notably e and π, which transcend other, merely algebraic, numbers, but we cannot appreciate their transcendence until we know about the algebraic ones, and what we learn with the latter remains true in our discussion of the transcendental ones. The same holds for sexuality.

It is a characteristic of living things, or *bionts*, that they are produced by and in turn produce similar bionts. My son has more or less the same shape as myself, he is of the same species. In some living species an individual directly produces new individuals like itself. The amoeba, for example, divides into two new individuals much the same as the parent; asexually reproducing yeast buds off new individuals much like the budding parent.

Our own species is different: I produced a *gamete* which fused with one from my wife to form that *soma*(plural: *somata*) which we call our son. We say that humans have a somatic *generation* and a gametic generation, alternating down the ages. A soma produces gametes; gametes fuse to form somata. This is a different use of the word *generation* from that employed by the historian, who commonly counts a whole life cycle under that name, whereas the biologist, some of the time, counts the forms, or kinds, of individual within a life cycle. Actually, of course, he often uses the word the same way as the historian, but here we need this specially biological concept.

In some species there are more than two generations: moss, for instance, has sporophytic, gametophytic and gametic generations; the flowering plant also has three: the rooted plant, heterospores(i.e. microspores, such as pollen, and macrospores) and gametes(the male gamete is produced by the microspore). If you are acquainted with the concept of ploidy, you will be interested to note that ploidy in moss generations does not parallel that in flowering-plant ones.

In the jellyfish, too, there are 3 generations: the sedentary polyp, the free-swimming medusa and the gamete. Some red algae(Rhodophyta) have 4: carposporophyte, tetrasporophyte, gametophyte and gamete.

A species may reproduce sometimes through a life cycle of generations and sometimes short-circuiting that cycle: the flowering plant sometimes exercises so-called *vegetative* reproduction, in which a rooted plant gives direct rise to another by cloning, runners, suckers, or the like. In principle, we might imagine, rather than life cycles, complex life networks, some generation yielding individuals of several distinct generations, but we do not in practice often find complicated networks.

An individual, or some member or organ of an individual, of some generation of a species may share vital matter with another member of the species for biological purposes. In the species we know, such sharing, called *conjugation*, is with members of the same generation: the gametophyte does not share with the sporophyte or the gamete. Also, in the life we know, conjugation is always between *two* members at a time, although that is not part of our definition of conjugation. The vital material shared may consist of genetic material(in our experience (de)oxyribonucleic acids arranged in chromosomes) or of individuals of another generation of the species, as when two human somata couple, transferring gametes from one to the other.

The participants in conjugation may fuse to form an individual of the next generation, or they may after conjugation continue their lives more or less independently, or they may cease to function, as when a pollen spore discharges gametes into the gynoecium of the "female" flower.

The structure of behaviour around conjugation is called *mating*. When two non-fusing individuals have an association longer than needed for mating, we call each the *mate* of the other.

The paramecium has only one generation, and individuals reproduce by fission. When conjugation occurs it does not automatically involve reproduction—indeed, there is no obvious connection, except that conjugation can take place only within the context of a species which continues to reproduce itself. We cannot say that reproduction is necessarily a purpose of conjugation.

When mating involves actual contact of conjugating non-fusing members we have *copulation*, distinct from the transportation of the vital material without contact of the members, as when an insect carries pollen from one flower to another.

Conjugation may happen without the shared material reaching either producer of the material. Somatic herring, for example, conjugate by releasing gametes into the sea, neither copulating nor themselves fusing. Whether we should say they mate depends on whether perception of the other conjugant causes release of the gametes. As the gametes may fuse with any of the right sex released by any member of the school, we can at most say that the school as a whole mates. It is better to say that it *spawns*.

We observe that members of a generation of some species conjugate non-randomly: the biological phenomenon of conjugation takes place among members of different *conjugal strain*s of the generation. When a paramecium splits to form two new paramecia, these are of the same conjugal strain and will not conjugate with each other; whenever two paramecia conjugate, each initiates a new conjugal strain.

Conjugation may also take place, as in somatic snails, between any two conjugation-apt members, but we do see conjugal strains in action in many species. Conjugation by members not grossly different, even in their strains if any, as in paramecium and the somatic snail, is called *syszygy*.

When members of the different conjugal strains are permanently differentiated for conjugation, with just as many strains in the generation as members engage in each conjugation, we call each strain a *sex*. When a generation conjugates by sex, we call the generation *sexual*.

When a generation does not itself copulate or fuse, as in the case of herring somata, we often nevertheless divide the generation into sexes, partitioning it according to the sex of the members of the next generation each member yields. Usually in such species we call the sexes of each generation by the same names as we use for the sexes in the generation produced. When a generation yields from one member members of all the sexes of the next generation, e.g. the tapeworm segment yielding both male and female gametes, we call the producing generation *hermaphrodite*.

How we name a sex is fairly arbitrary. The names given to human somatic sexes are used for human gametes produced by the respective somatic sexes, by homology for the gametes of other species, and so for other generations of those species. Where homology is difficult, we may use perhaps far-fetched analogy to human somata, and for some species we use quite different names.

When we call all generations of a species sexual, we also call the species *sexual*. When we call only some of the generations sexual, as in the case of moss, we say that the species exhibits *alternation of generations*.

The fusing of two gametes to form an individual of the next generation is called *fertilization*. It is one form of *conception*, the process by which one generation gives rise to the next. The conception of human gametes is by a process, within certain tissues of the soma, called *meiosis*. The jellyfish medusa has its conception in *budding* from the polyp. I rather suspect that not all modes of conception have names yet.

Because a human soma is in fact conceived, i.e. has its conception, at fertilization, we often use "conception" to mean fertilization, but it seems better to distinguish the concepts and to state(falsifiably) as a fact that human conception is at fertilization, occurs at fertilization, or is fertilization.

Excursus 1

Although the "generation" terminology was not used, medieval biology described the human life cycle as occurring in more than the modern 2 generations(cf. Dante: *Commedia* 2(*Purgatorio*):25:34-75). Instead of gametes, the scientists of those times thought that copulation brought two sexes of a *liquid* form together in fertilization. The merging of these caused the conception of a *vegetable* form, i.e. a very symmetric form, without organized or organizing centres. In this there eventually budded an *animal*, or *sensitive*, generation, which absorbed the remains of the vegetable. The animal eventually, around the third month after fertilization, gave rise to the *rational* generation, although whether this conception should be called budding is unclear to me—the rational took over the animal as the animal did the vegetable.

It was because of this biology that people used to distinguish early abortion from murder. When Harvey and others in the 17th century showed that the rational or somatic form had its conception at fertilization, early abortion too became condemned as murder, although legislatures often retained the three-months rule inherited from the now obsolete biology.

I believe that people ignorant of science in the Middle Ages and even earlier had an opinion nearer to modern theory than to the science of their days, but that discussion would lead us far afield.

End of Excursus 1

Governing the conjugal or mating behaviour of each member of a conjugal generation is a set of reflexes, habits, instincts and so on. We call these tendencies *erotic*, and the whole combination of them constitutes the member's *eroticism*. In an organism with more than a certain development of the nervous system we recognise a psychology of eroticism. The human soma is the measure of all things, at least when the human soma is doing the measuring, but the human soma is a very complex organism and psyche, and it is probably a good idea to understand as much as possible of eroticism in simpler organisms before uttering far-reaching judgements about the behaviour appropriate for the human soma.

Among a member's erotic tendencies are those which determine the characteristics of the members with which it seeks to conjugate. For example, some men have a strong attraction to red-headed women, some are repelled by potential conjugal partners of a different race, and so on. We may say that for any detectable characteristic each member has a component of attraction, whether negative, zero or positive. The various components may not combine linearly or even monotonically(it might be that a man is attracted by red hair on a woman only if she wears dark clothes, say). In a generation with strains, a positive component towards members of different strains is natural, i.e. belongs to the biological nature of the situation, and, to use a slightly loaded word, healthy; a negative component is presumably disordered. The specialization involved implies that such a negative component in a sexual form is always disordered, regardless of its cause or rectifiability. Besides the disorder implicit even in a potentially syszygous form with conjugal strains, it constitutes an instinct for syszygy in an organism anatomically and physiologically incapable of syszygy. An ideologically unfashionable but conceptually correct name for a negative sexual component in the eroticism is *sexual inversion*, applied either to the eroticism or to the individual(or member). By such analysis of conjugation in general we can derive criteria for judging the health of the form of most interest to us, viz. the somatic human.

By extension, we call behaviour of such forms as the herring soma erotic when it has relevance to the release of gametes. There may be(I do not know) pheromones which induce release of gametes when a member of the other somatic sex is ready to release; such information may provide a basis on which to understand the behaviour of amphibia, whose somata co-operate to share vital material externally, and then of animals which actually copulate in the strict sense.

Experiencing erotic urges, an organism may conjugate or, in observable circumstances, simulate conjugation. In particular, organisms which have bodies for copulation may actually copulate or may simulate copulation. Such simulation, especially when it involves bodily reactions similar to those experienced in conjugation, is called *masturbation*. Masturbation may be solitary, concerted, or mutual. It may occur with members of the other sex of the generation, with those of the same sex, with quite different organisms—observation will tell us what in fact occurs in what circumstances in any species. Whatever value conjugation may have(not discussed here), simulated conjugation is probably(but we need observation and further reasoning to be sure) a disorder in behaviour, presumably resulting from some disorder in the erotic impulses or, in an organism with a definite mind, the reason.

Understanding the biology of conjugality in general and sexuality in particular, we can fairly easily conclude that non-sexual eroticism is unhealthy in a sexual animal. Exactly how important it is we can leave for the psychologists(who, we hope, will describe on the basis of physiology) and moralists(who, we hope, will describe on the basis of physiology and sound psychology).

Excursus 2

Some particularly misleading terminology centres around the word *homosexual*. This word and its co-relatives occur in 3 distinct meaning spaces, and people frequently confuse the meanings. What is said usually needs to be restated in consistent terminology before judgement can be made.

Space 1.

A set of members of a sexual generation may be of the same or of varied sexes. If they are of the same sex, we call the set *homosexual*; if they are of several sexes we call the set *heterosexual.* We talk, for instance, of homosexual and heterosexual twins. If we say "Leslie is homosexual" we mean that Leslie is of the same sex as someone we are already thinking of, and similarly for "Evelyn is heterosexual". By slight extension we can talk of actions of members of the same sex as homosexual(at one time in Europe, at least among the better-off, smoking was a homosexual activity), and actions of members of different sexes may be called heterosexual. In this meaning space, copulation is of logical necessity heterosexual.

Space 2.

A member of a sexual generation has an erotic component concerning the conjugal attractiveness of members of another sex. If the component is positive we call the member *heterosexual,* if zero *bisexual,* if negative *homosexual.* In this meaning space, anything bisexual is neither heterosexual nor homosexual.

Space 3.

Conjugation in a sexual generation is called *heterosexual;* so are simulated copulation, alias mutual masturbation, and concerted masturbation, when the participants are of different sexes. Mutual and concerted masturbation by members of the same sex is called *homosexual.* We call individuals *heterosexual* or *homosexual* as they participate in heterosexual or homosexual activities. We call them *bisexual* if they are both heterosexual **and** homosexual, in contrast to the meaning in Space 2.

It may seem that Space 1 is little used, but in fact careful observation of speech reveals that it turns up quite often, running misleadingly into the other spaces. There is between spaces 2 and 3 none of the often assumed parallelism between 'homosexual and heterosexual tendencies' and 'homosexual and heterosexual actions' indicating that the popular concept *homosexuality* is improper—so that homophobia and homosexualism, two sets of behaviours towards the concept, are irrational, vanishing as the concept dissolves under lexical criticism. Let us now look at some related words, also liable to confusion.

The word *gay* has at least 3 meanings. "Leslie is gay" can mean

a. Leslie is irresponsibly happy and carefree(Martial is so described for his sexual promiscuity in the introduction to my copy of his works)

or

b. Leslie is homosexual-2, i.e. sexually inverted, and willing to be homosexual-3, i.e. willing to engage in concerted or mutual masturbation

or

c. Leslie is gay-b and male.

The word *Lesbian* is very ambiguous. It can mean:

a. belonging to or associated with Lesbos, an island in the Aegean Sea, whose main town is and for a long time has been Mytilene

or

b. a Lesbian rule, i.e. a tape measure, allegedly invented by someone who was Lesbian-a

or

c. a woman poet, especially if the speaker holds that her poetry is good, in memory of a colony of women poets, led by one Sappho, who a long time ago lived on Lesbos

or

d. a woman who is homosexual-2

or

e. a woman who is homosexual-3

or

f. a woman who is gay-b.

End of Excursus 2

I leave as an exercise for the reader the complete listing of the meanings of the word *sex*.

rev.1999.04.20

HANGWITE IN CONTEXT

God endows all men with inalienable dignity, consisting mainly of such rights as those to life, to liberty and to property. These rights do not derive from the state: we have them even where there is no state, or government, in the usual sense. We can distinguish between a "state of nature", which must be how humanity started, and which today still arises from time to time, and a "state of government", in which we have such institutions as judges and executors of the law.

The basic human rights may be forfeited by violating them in others: we are all aware that a criminal may justly be deprived by the state of his property, his liberty and, in extreme cases, his life. A violator of human rights may also justly be punished in such ways where there is no government. Such punishment I call *hangwite*. It is distinct from the obtention of redress for a violation, e.g. by taking from a thief goods equal in value to those he has stolen or destroyed. Hangwite is also distinct from damaging someone in compelling him to do right, e.g., give up stolen goods, refrain from murder or robbery. By hangwite an actual punishment is inflicted. Those whose rights are violated have the right to redress; in a state of nature anyone has the right to execute hangwite.

Because hangwite can lead to vendettas and other injustice, governments are established for the securing of human rights. When governments punish, they should do so with an objective declaration that the criminal has forfeited his right. Two great advantages of government are that the violator can be punished more leniently than in a state of nature, where death is often the only practical punishment, and that matters can be righted which are not important enough for anyone in a state of nature to bother righting, though their cumulative effect may be great.

In the primitive stages of government, and when government cannot act(due, say, to isolation or emergency), individuals retain the right of hangwite. As government develops, it not only protects human rights but restores them to a punished criminal, even though he might rightly have suffered more severe punishment. The developing state of government tries to purge itself gentle with humane statute, improving the accuracy and justice of punishment by proceeding consistently with trials and punishing indirect violations of human rights, something unjust to do without prior statute. Our right to security from indirect violations is a civil right rather than a basic human right.

Another civil right is that to trial before punishment. As government becomes secure in its punishment of criminals, the supposed criminal obtains by statute of some kind the civil right to due process, and unnecessary hangwite becomes a crime. In England under Edward the Confessor, the punishment for this violation of a civil right was a fine of ten shillings; it is worthy of note that the fine was twenty shillings if the punisher was a government officer: the purpose of government being to secure human rights, sometimes by building around the basic rights the fence of civil rights, it is worse for a government officer than for someone else to violate rights. At a still later stage the government rightly punishes almost all hangwite as though the punished criminal had been an innocent victim. I here repeat that hangwite is distinct from injuring someone in defence of people or property.

In punishing hangwite, the judge should take into account the perpetrator's chance of getting the violator to court, as well as the certainty of the perpetrator's knowledge of the guilt of the punished person. If the government neglects to punish some definite violation of a basic human right, e.g. abortion in many countries today or suttee in pre-British India, it may not justly punish hangwite in relation to such violations. The perpetrator of hangwite in such cases may reasonably hope(though perhaps not expect) to be acquitted of crime, because the government has not arranged itself to execute the punishment. A judge who punishes hangwite in such circumstances, even though he may seem bound by statute and precedent to do so, is an unjust judge.

Another distinction to make here is between hangwite and *rebellion*. Rebellion is the attempt to change the government by force rather than by its own constitutional procedures. The perpetrator of hangwite may have the defence that the government is failing in its duty at a fundamental level and so must let him do the work of justice; the rebel is trying to overthrow the government which appoints the judge, not to supplement the government, and cannot reasonably hope that the judge will recognize the justice of the attempt. "Mr magistrate", said Mohandas Gandhi once, "It's your duty to send me to prison".

I have mentioned abortion and suttee because their impunity in some legal systems makes them clear examples. More difficulty arises when we have to do with governments which have the procedures for punishing a crime but fail to do so, as in the murder of Eula Love. To recognize hangwite we need to know whether it would occur in a state of nature, and surely many minor crimes would not be punished at all in a state of nature. We also need to be approximately as certain as the government's courts, did they take cognizance, would be of the guilt of the supposed violator. In the Eula Love case those grounds are given, though I think that perhaps by now a morally binding stature of limitations has intervened.

For such cases of government inactivity, whether by neglect or refusal, it may be legitimate to form *death squads* of hangwite heroes, filling in where the government is not doing its duty. When the government's refusal to punish the violation seems to justify hangwite, the reason behind such refusal must be taken into account: is it general corruption of government officers, forgetting the purpose of government, as protected the murderers of Eula Love, or some well-intentioned and somehow justifiable mercy? The hangwite heroes must be sure of this, as well as of the facts of the actual case. Also, the violation they choose to punish must be a direct violation of rights, not of some governmental regulation fencing the basic human rights.

Most of the death squads of Central America are illegitimate, for they kill organizers of institutions they do not like but which the death-dealers have no right of themselves to prohibit, and which the government itself does not prohibit. Even where the government does prohibit some organization, presumably rightly, mere participation in the organization is not a violation of basic rights and therefore not liable to hangwite.

It is possible that death squads may be justified(I do not think any of the Central American ones have been for a long time) as a kind of rebellion not to overthrow the government but to make up for its wrong-headedness. This is at least conceivable but members of such death squads may not reasonably hope for acquittal on the grounds of justice of their cause.

Many death squads, such as the largest until recently in El Salvador, are rebels: they seek to *change* the government violently. If the government has the consent of the people, which it must always be held to have when democratically elected and within its electoral term and constitutional limitations, rebellion is always wrong. It would be wrong of captured rebels to allege hangwite as a defence. The same is true of rebellion even against a dictatorship, except for particular instances of rebel action, but it is spiritually dangerous to try to be a rebel and a hangwite hero at once. To be either may also, of course, be imprudent.

1996.03.04

THE MEANINGS OF 'ISRAEL'

Truth, Justice and peace, and in that order, says some mishna. Truth means being symbolically and factually correct, new facts sending us back to our use of words(and other symbols) to ensure that we are indeed symbolically correct. People talk a lot of rubbish through being symbolically incorrect and in particular they talk a lot of rubbish about the Holy Land by ambiguous use of the name *Israel,* a word with many meanings. In such a situation we must be humble, diligent, patient, honest and courageous enough to relearn and rearrange what we thought we already knew. The names *Jew* and *Arab* also have some ambiguity of occasional importance in discussion of the Holy Land question set, but I propose here to deal only with *Israel,* characterizing each known referent(or referent set). The necessary distinctions made, we can bring our attention to bear on the real issues involved without the emotional reactions which commonly stultify reason. Thus we may map the way to Justice and on to Peace(political correctness?). However I plan here to give only a few examples where ambiguity has misled, not solve the entire problem set today.

I start by listing the known(to me) characterizations.

1a. Jacob son of Isaac son of Abraham who gained this name("God will struggle",) by struggling with[an angel of] God[1].

1b. Any supposed person named, more or less directly, after #1a, e.g.:

    i. Professor Shahak of HUJ;

    ii. Guy, the Cambridge astronomer;

    iii. one of the sons of Seljuq;

    iv. a Korean in my Hebrew class.

1c. Any person held to be struggling spiritually with God, fate or circumstances,

2a. The spiritual descent of #1a. This people became a nation(Hebrew: *goy*) in Egypt[2]; they left Egypt, passing Sinai, where they ceased to be a nation[3], remaining(or perhaps becoming) a church(Hebrew: *qahal*). When God calls them a nation he is annoyed with them(with one odd exception[4]).

2b. Any coherent proper subset of #2a, especially considered as central to #2a. The millions of examples include:

   i. #2a from the time of Moses until the Common Era;

   ii. Those who at least implicitly recognize the authority of the Council of Jerusalem[5]; these are commonly called "Christians";

   iii. Those who at least implicitly recognize the authority of the Council of Jamnia;

   iv. The Samaritans

   v. The Catholic Church

   vi. The members of the churches of the Southern Baptist Conference;

   vii. All the Hasidim of Square Town;

   viii. The Catholics of Stourbridge and environs;

   ix. The members of the members of the Stourbridge Council of Churches.

2c. Any community or cause whose success is for the nonce held to be desirable.

3. The Davidic Kingdom as a state and as a citizenry, or territorial society, extending before and after David in time, especially as a citizenry, less clearly as a state.

4. The state founded around Jeroboam[6] as #3 collapsed.

5. Eretz Israel, Eretz Canaan, Palestine, the Holy Land; it has the name[7] for being the place of early development of #2.

6. The Israeli state, the Zionist state, Herzl's Judenstaat, with extension to citizenry, intended as an instrument of #2b(iii) and placed in #5.

7a. The territory acquired by #6 in 1948.

7b. The territory assigned to #6 by a particular partition plan.

7c. The territory over which #6 at a particular time holds sway.

7d. The territory which #6 at a particular time rules directly.

7e. The territory in which #6 at a particular time exercises domestic Jurisdiction.

Some multivalency in speech is inevitable and legitimate. For instance, #2a and #3 for a long time had the same membership, which usually did not distinguish church and state. However, even with identical membership, church and state have different functions and often should be distinguished.

The various territorial meanings are often carelessly confused. When someone talks of going from Jezzine to "Israel proper" he recognizes that Jezzine is in #7c, but is he distinguishing this from #5, #7a, #7d or #7e? If someone talks of going from the Golan Heights to "Israel proper" is he recognizing them as being in #7c or #7d, and is he distinguishing this from #5 or #7a?

Other confusions of meaning are more important. I once saw in the *Los Angeles Times* an advertisement for the *Fncyclopaedia Judaica* with a picture of Golda Meir telling us "If you buy this encyclopaedia for your children, Israel will live for ever". But Meir was a high leader of #6, and we buy our children encyclopaedias in the hope that some #2b will live forever. Does the Baptist governor of a mainly Baptist state have a special status in recommending religious literature to Baptists in a largely Catholic conurbation? Perhaps, but it would be illegitimate to suppose any deep link between the welfare of his state and that of the local church far away from that state—at least, any such link should be explicitly justified. Meir was saying in effect "You love #2b(iii), so have Congress arm #6"; such an implication should be explicitated and analyzed, not supposed on the coincidence of names.

A stranger, and more important, confusion is that made by President Clinton when, like President Carter before him, he says that promises made by God to #2a in general and #2b(i) in particular, with perhaps some reference to #3, should be fulfilled in #2b(iii) and #6. If he had thought a little, President Carter should surely have decided that promises to #2a should be fulfilled centrally in #2b(vi); if he had known the relevant history, the same thought should have led him to suppose that any promise to #3 must be fulfilled in the PLO, i.e., by his own announced principles he should change sides in the quarrel for political rule in the Holy Land. He shares this mainly linguistic misunderstanding with many other people in the United States and elsewhere.

We who care about the Holy Land question set must beware of these ambiguities and ourselves avoid them. My preference is to use clear phrases rather than the name "Israel" for #6 and #7. Despite biblical warrant, I also like to avoid it for #5, chiefly because of the confusion Zionism has brought to this meaning. Indeed, it is even worth the bother of distinguishing #3 from #4 by saying "the Davidic Kingdom" and "the northern Kingdom of Israel" most of the time. Confusions among the other meanings are rare and usually resolvable without rancor.

I note that the non-nationality of #2a and by implication of every #2b, although clearly biblically important, seems not to have been explored by Christian scholars, although Jamnia Jews are for the most part well aware of it, while willing to fudge to mislead outsiders(and the intelligent will understand). The point may have some importance for the understanding and solution of the problem set. Certainly distinguishing the various meanings listed above will aid understanding.

KINDS OF RACIALISM

So many things are called *racism* or *racialism* that we can quite easily get lost in deciding whether a particular phenomenon is indeed a kind of racialism, or immoral, or real, or even properly imaginable. The situation is not made easier by certain United Nations documents which include a definition of *Apartheid* quite different from that published and practised by the South African Nationalists, inventors of the term. There are similar difficulties elsewhere, besides a frequent confusion of a real personal ideal, the ideal expressed and the ideal affirmed by action—this is what happened with the UN regarding Apartheid: the word gurus confused these three absurdly. Distinction here would have been helpful, as will be seen later.

Another problem is confusion with *racial discrimination*. I give 4 casuses of racial discrimination which we would be hesitant to call racialism.

Casus 1. A Christian priest goes into a shop in Birmingham's Soho. If the person behind the counter is black or white, the priest speaks English; if brown, he speaks Punjabi, in which, as a good Birmingham Priest, he is of course fluent. The priest is certainly discriminating by race, but is he a racialist?

Casus 2. A GP examines two male patients complaining of difficulty passing urine. She asks questions, prods them, does a PR on each and suspects prostatoma. She writes the lab a note asking for a prostate biopsy on each. The lab tells her that under the new improved NHS rationing system she has only one prostate biopsy left this fiscal year. Which is it to be? Both men are in similar family and employment situations, apparently equally moral and imaginative and so forth. One is Afro and one Euro. Statistics indicate that Afro men are twice as likely to die of prostatoma as

Euro ones, so the Afro man gets the biopsy and the Euro one has to wait for next fiscal year. Is she a racialist?

Casus 3. A DP manager needs two contract programmers, one for 6 months and one for 4 months. He has three applicants: one Oriental, one Euro, one Afro. He does not have much time to evaluate them, and their credentials seem equivalent. He knows that on average in the U.S. Orientals do best at analysis tests and Afros worst. So the Oriental gets the 6-month contract and the Euro gets the 4-month one. Is the manager a racialist?

Casus 4. When the Afro Skinheads of London go Queer-bashing they sometimes let a Euro Queer pass, but they always bash an Afro Queer, because he's letting the side down. Are they racialists?

Let us look at definitions of racialism. The OED tells us that *racism* sometimes refers to theory of race(the relationship between Alsatians and Dachshunds, I suppose), some kind of science; and that the word is also a synonym for *racialism*, which refers to ideals regarding usually human race and methods of realizing such ideals. So I choose the less ambiguous *racialism*. Alas, the OED's definition does not include Apartheid, because Apartheid assumes that all races—'groups' in Nationalist terminology—are at least in principle of equal worth, nor Zionism, which chooses a community to terminate, not to exalt, which is what the OED definition would require. A definition of racialism not covering Apartheid would be aberrant.

I prefer this definition: "It is the notion of ascribing moral, social or political significance to a man's genetic lineage—the notion that a man's intellectual and characterological traits are produced and transmitted by his internal body chemistry…that a man is to be judged, not by his own character and actions, but by the character and actions of a collective of ancestors"(Ayn Rand: *Virtue of Selfishness* ch. 17 par.2). Rand goes on with improbable causes of racialism(she says *racism*, but never mind that), and we can safely ignore the rest of the chapter, but her definition is better than that of the OED. It is still not quite what we want: when the Euro

Skinhead bashes a Paki he is not claiming that Auden is superior to Tagore, Rutherford to Bose, Edward I to Babur.

The activities I wish to classify ascribe not only by race but by various other collectivizations: group, race, nation, tribe, ethnicity, nationality, people, caste... Perhaps we should confine *racialism* to ascription by actual biological race, but then we could not call the Paki-bashing Skinhead a racialist, because his *Paki* includes his fellow-Aryans the Afghans, and the non-Aryan Tamils. The Nazis did try to be scientific, but classified quite at odds with the biological reality, even apart such *ad hoc* hypocrisy as calling Japanese "Aryan". Again, the two communities in Northern Ireland, if we go back a few centuries, surely have large proportions of common ancestry.

A further problem arises with the use of such negatively defined words as *wog*, *Black* as British social workers use it, *foreigner*, *non*-anything, etc. Socrates pointed out long ago that an Italian and an Egyptian had nothing in common they did not share with a Greek, but both, not being Greeks, were called wogs. I propose to use instead of *race* the Arabic-derived word *qaum*, common to several languages spoken in Britain, signifying a set of people who stand together. Whether they stand together of their own accord, by co-incidence of some specific quality, or merely by the ignorance of others, is irrelevant: this stand-in for race is in the eyes of the racialist.

I wish to classify the various ideals of ascribing moral and especially political significance to a person's qaum rather than to his own character, ability and other properties. In casuses 1, 2 and 3 above we have what seem to be correctible evaluations of persons on the basis of their race; a racialist makes his criterion independent of facts he may learn about any particular person.

He loves his qaum best who strives to make it best. Such is the *patriot*, whom we now recognize in Casus 4, whatever we may think of his method of improving his qaum. Other styles of patriotism emphasize self-respect of the qaum, not exposing its problems to other qaums—"not in front of the natives", as the colonial ladies used to say.

As *racialism* has pejorative connotations, we may want to confine it in practice to the harsher forms of *qaumism*, say, but the degree and nature of harshness involved would be difficult to define and should not in any case be applied until we have a clear classification so that we can apply the harshness criterion similarly in all the kinds. Racialists by and large do not do that, but I do not make the Devil my example. Racialists frequently confuse their ideal, their justification thereof and their motivations for holding that ideal. I am not here discussing the "real" motivation of each kind of racialism(think of the variety of motives behind Zionism), and when someone is differently racialist in different situations(e.g. the Zulu chauvinist regarding KwaZulu and Soweto) I want to characterize his conflicting ideals separately. This is not a psychology(nor a morality) exercise.

The first division I propose is between those racialisms which identify qaum with citizenry and those which seek for a qaum some place in relation to a citizenry. I live in the English West Midlands. If I were a Welsh Nationalist I would at the last general election have voted for the Liberal Democrat candidate, because his party was that most likely to erect a Welsh homeland state. If I were a Welsh tribalist I would have voted for the Labour Candidate, because his party leader was Welsh and I would want power for someone of my tribe throughout the citizenry. I think I have here accurately defined the difference we in practice make between *tribalism* and *nationalism*. Sometimes we have to distinguish this meaning of *nationalism* from territorial theories of the ideal political subdivision of humanity, but that should rarely be important. A particular racialism may require recognition of sub-qaums and sub-citizenries.

1. *Nationalism* identifies qaum and citizenry ideally and attempts to make them identical actually. It rejects the possibility of a multinational citizenry. It can be total, as in South African Apartheid as originally envisaged, or partial, as some people would like to see

evolve in the new South Africa; such people tend to be tribalist furth of their homeland. There are 2 nationalist ideals: *Apartheid* and *assimilationism*.

1.1 *Apartheid* says that if there are many qaums there must be many citizenries. Action affirmative of this ideal includes discrimination in residence and settlement policies, in employment, in civil abilities and in education.

a. South African Apartheid arose as a reaction to the mixing of various races under a policy of White Supremacy. Many minor and some major restrictions, often inherited from White Supremacy, were placed on people, mainly Bantu, living outside their assigned territories, and they were encouraged to migrate to those territories.

b. The New Africa movement in the United States wants the U.S. to cede to an Afro-American polity several states, to compensate all the White people in those states for their expulsion to the remaining states, and to reward Afros for migrating to the ceded states. New Africa should for at least two decades receive generous foreign aid from the U.S. as compensation for the sufferings of slavery and White Supremacy. There is usually little concern for other qaums, but sometimes one sees the suggestion that there be also a Jewish state, in the New York City area.

c. Theresienstadt was a short-lived Nazi project of permanent shtetls for those classified as Jews. The previous inhabitants of a town were expelled and the Führer kindly presented the Jews with it, mainly because of their failure to participate in Zionism and migrate to some land outside Europe. The plan was abandoned in favour of mass murder of the allegedly poisonous qaum.

1.2 *Assimilationism* also rejects the multinational citizenry: as there is but one citizenry, there must be but one qaum. Action affirmative of this principle consists mainly of decreeing and enforcing quotas for each qaum, in proportion to local or citizenry-wide population sizes, in much the same fields as are involved for Apartheid. One qaum is generally held to be normative, and the intention is that the others become more and more like it, until their distinctive traits, barring trivia, become lost.

    a. Affirmative Action in the United States is usually for assimilation: all the Niggers and Dagoes must become black Honkies(Oreos) and brown Gringos(cocos) respectively. It is often attempted to justify Affirmative Action as compensation for the wrongs suffered by Afros under White Supremacy(neatly fitting Rand's definition regarding a 'collective of ancestors'), but it does sometimes happen that Afros are not the ones preferentially employed, and those who favour Affirmative Action usually oppose tax credits for church schooling, which might upgrade Afros *en masse* without Waspifying them.

    b. In India members of the lower or 'scheduled' castes are often preferred for public service over better qualified members of higher castes. The principle is as in the U.S., with much the same attempted justification.

2. *Tribalism* seeks special status in the citizenry for some qaum, or set of qaums. This kind of racialism is much more common than Nationalism among the movements traditionally described(or, more precisely, condemned) as racialist, but that may be an accident of linguistic history. Tribalism is usually aimed at the ascendancy of one qaum over the others in the citizenry, i.e. at making members of the qaum leaders of the citizenry and having those in power favour members of the qaum. Alternatively, there may be a complete theory of qaum relationship within the citizenry. Again, one qaum may be specially classed as a *de*scendancy. Finally, a qaum may be excluded from the citizenry.

2.1 *Ascendancy* is the commonest kind of tribalism. It is often qualified with 'in our country' or the like, which may make it seem Nationalism, but the Tribalist wants power for his tribe outside its homeland too. The Scottish Nationalist is often a Scottish Tribalist in Britain as a whole, affronted if forbidden to enter areas of Britain outside his homeland.

a. The British Empire was run on the theory of ascendancy of British or at least European people in each colony. So instinctive can this claim be that in hearing of some non-European people's life one is on the lookout for the European District Commissioner or the like to take charge and sort things out in time of difficulty—this happened to me when I watched *Kismet* in the 1950s, but the Governor or whatever never showed up. It should not have happened to me, because I was a Christian and consciously believed in the equality of all people regardless of race, but explicit doctrines are not the only ones imbibed.

b. European Christian missions sent home what amounted to reactions to the imperial theory: the Christians in Europe were told, and often believed, that non-White people were, despite not yet being Christian, in may ways better than the Whites ruling them. This belief is still strong among Euros. In the 1950s the belief led to popular British support for Mau Mau; in the 1960s Europeans were somehow to blame for all the woes of Africa.

c. In many African states people vote by qaum rather than by ideology. In Somalia, Kenya and South Africa there are alliances among qaums(or among supposedly representative members of qaums) such that members of one qaum will vote for candidates from the alliance, not just their own qaum. Thus we have a Zulu-Afrikaner alliance in Inkatha, something rather more complicated in the ANC, and so forth.

d. In Malaysia there is a government policy of preference for Malays over other races(this policy led to the secession of Singapore) in commerce and education. The policy is variously justified as a means of permanent ascendancy of the Malays in their own country and as an upgrade to bring them, whatever individual merit may be involved, to the same average prosperity as the Indians and Chinese.

2.2 *Total systems* are sometimes attempted. In the British Empire there was sometimes an implicit hierarchy of qaums, e.g. in Kenya Europeans above Asians above Africans. But the set of attitudes among Europeans may have been rather different: Asians are sly, Africans stupid. A further difficulty might arise in classification by reason of patriotism mixed in: an Afrikaner thought it dreadful that one European scold another in the presence of an African, and not merely because the Afrikaner thought Europeans superior to Africans.

   a. Hindu India had an ideal of four qaums called *varna*s or *caste*s, with a definite pecking order, most recently: Brahmin, Kshatriya, Vaisya, Shudra. Within each varna were lower-level qaums called *jati*s, each again with a pecking order, or perhaps a pecking lattice or pecking graph. The lowest Shudra jati was of the Pariahs, whose name Europeans mistakenly used for those of no varna, of whom more at 2.4a.

   b. Nazi theory seems to have had an explicit place(in or out) for every qaum imaginable. At the top were the German races(Nordic, Falian, etc.), under them other non-Slavic Europeans, then non-European Aryans. Slavs and Negroes were to be hewers of wood and drawers of water(did Vlassilov know this?), both carefully watched, Slavs because of inborn nastiness, Negroes because of faultless brutishness. Nazi theory changed, so what I here say may not fit every official utterance and action.

   c. The British Empire employed Indians as administrators in Africa, yielding the European-Asian-African pyramid I mentioned earlier.

2.3 *Descendancy* is the name I have chosen for the ideal that some qaum be held inferior to others in the citizenry, independent of the relationships of those other qaums among themselves.

a. In Eastern Europe there was often a plethora of qaums in a city or other district: Germans, various kinds of Slavs, Magyars, what-have-you. There is a tradition among Eastern European Jews that their qaum was always despised by all the others, who would join forces against a Jew despite any differences among themselves.

b. Among Israelis there is, apart from the native population and non-"Jewish" immigrant groups, tremendous variety of qaum. There is a complex pecking order: the stratification, like that among the British social classes, is such that there is always someone to look down upon. Unless one is an Indian: they are at the bottom of every other qaum's system.

2.4 *Exclusion* of a qaum totally from the citizenry is distinct from, but often joined with, other tribalisms. Sometimes a citizenry is to exclude some qaum not because an ascendant qaum is all-important but because the excluded qaum is all-repulsive.

a. In Hindu India the Brahmin and Kshatriya must have regard for the good of the other varnas, but they need and should have no regard for outcastes. So little concern is given to them that we generally refer to them by the mistaken *Pariah*, or the 20th-century euphemisms *Antyajat* and *Harijan*; they nowadays often call themselves *Dalit*, i.e. downtrodden. The historically proper term is *Chandala*, from pre-Aryan times. Until the Union of India decreed otherwise they might not enter temples. Cynically, one might find some use for them, but not in the ideal scheme of things.

b. Nazis excluded Jews and Gypsies from their ideal stratified citizenry, initially by Apartheid(1.1c) and, when that failed, by mass murder. A Nazi might in the goodness of his heart provide for the needs of Slavs and Negroes, knowing better what they needed than they in their subhumanity could well express, but not for Jews.

c. In 1903 the World Zionist Congress chose Palestinians not classed as (Jamnia) Jews as worthy of being cast out of any citizenry. When Golda Meir said "There never was a Palestinian People" she was talking rubbish historically, but she was expressing a fundamental truth about Zionism. This is not setting up a pecking order, something the Israelis to some extent do with non-Jew non-Palestinians in the land: it is a rejection of a qaum as unworthy of citizenship at any level. The extent to which mass murder rather than assimilation to other qaums is appropriate is a divisive question among Zionists.

Any racialist is likely to be unclear about his racial ideals and his dreams of his citizenry. I have here tried to set things out systematically, but racialism does not arise by systematic thought, although people do sometimes try to develop systematically some of the ideas they already have. Careful thought from the basis of Afrikaner fear of assimilation of the Bantu to the Rooineks, for instance, led to the Apartheid dream, something many of the Afrikaners voting Nationalist did not really expect, and something some of them never wholeheartedly embraced, clinging, but with different details, to the White Supremacy which had threatened them with an over-abundance of Anglophones; nevertheless, it was wrong of opponents to identify Apartheid with White Supremacy, and probably made the forty-year effort worse for all concerned than it would otherwise have been.

Sticking with examples in South Africa, we often see such mixing of ideals as this: someone is a Zulu nationalist in that he wants KwaZulu to continue as an almost exclusively Zulu polity or citizenry, but outside the homeland he is a Zulu tribalist, wanting Zulus, possibly in *ad hoc* coalitions, to form the ascendancy. This is not even a contradictory mixture, although many mixtures are.

At the lowest level in my analysis I might have given many further examples, e.g. the forms of assimilation used for some time within the French and Portuguese empires. I suspect that assimilationism may admit finer classification.

A great advantage of this kind of analysis is that it helps us understand that our use of *racialism* or *racism* is often more pejorative than descriptive. We have a tendency not to use these terms for practices and policies of which we approve. I once horrified a young U.S.American by showing him the parallels between 1.1a and 1.2a. He kept on repeating "You're talking about two entirely different things", but I was the only one of us to make any distinction between them. He had been taught that Apartheid was something detestable done in a far-off land while the Affirmative Action of his own country was a laudable and even generous policy of his own race. With a little objectivity we can see that the policies are not only morally identical but remarkably similar in origin—something for the political scientist to note.

Similarly, if we condemn, as I do, the pro-Apartheid or provisionally pro-Apartheid Zulu nationalist for insisting that his neighbor's children be educated through Zulu rather than through English, we are in reason bound to condemn the Welsh chauvinist for a similar demand. This demonstrates something else important in political morality: if we condemn some wickedness in a far place we must surely condemn it also in a near place. Good politics goes beyond home, but it must start there.

A third value in this analysis is that it shows us horrors we had not noticed. We rightly condemn the exclusion of Palestinians from certain Israeli university departments; we must also condemn the preference for Malays, in defiance of academic merit, in admission to Malaysian university courses, even though we may think the Israeli motive worse—for it the *action* against which we protest.

Analysis may, finally, be of use in converting the racialist. A racialist of one kind, whether or not he admits the description for himself, frequently condemns other kinds. On the occasions when he is willing to listen, we can, by use of honest and largely non-judgemental analysis, hold up to him a probably unpleasant mirror.

1995.08.09

Motives of Zionism

When discussing Zionism, perhaps more than any other political question set, people get highly annoyed at the stupidity of their interlocutors. As usual, there are linguistic problems behind this frustration and, as usual, those involved refuse to consider that their language may be at all ambiguous or otherwise erroneous. They all assume a certain set of motives to be self-evidently legitimate, but are shy of analyzing or even explicitating them. This is especially so for Zionism because quite often one side is not candid about its motives, leaving the intelligent to understand. I propose here to list some important motives for Zionism: there is a large set of differing motives which happen to issue in common action, skilfully steered by those with one of the motives, but often, due to the co-incidence of action, not requiring explicit steering.

First let us be clear what we mean by Zionism: we are not talking about *any* assignment of territory to a church; Kahnawata, Nagasaki and Square Town are not our concern. I understand Zionism, the 'true' Zionism, to be the political, cultural, social and religious movement nowadays so called, with some kind of emotive and often organizational continuity from David Alroy to David Ben-Gurion, to put Eretz Israel alias Palestine alias the Holy Land under Jewish settlement and rule; it became organized in the World Zionist Organization about the beginning of this century, with such organizational off-shoots as the Jewish National Fund, the Jewish Agency for Palestine and the Israeli State. It must be distinguished from those movements, also called Zionist, which organized settlements of Jews in Argentina in the last century, and even from the ideals of Theodor Herzl, founder of the Organization but a late-comer to the movement, for he by no means insisted on Eretz Israel.

60

But just what is a *Jew* within Zionist terminology? We often call the followers of Moses Jews, even before they followed Moses. This is a loose use of the name, for among the spiritual followers of Moses we find the Samaritans, who, we are told, have nothing to do with Jews[1]. Thus we have a second meaning for the name: those adhering to the doctrinal recension of Ezra, one branch of the following of Moses, the other well-known one being the Samaritans, with the Yemenites a third. Early in the Common Era, those following Ezra split: the Council of Jerusalem crystallized Christendom as one branch, and the Council of Jamnia crystallized the rabbinical tradition; the Falashas may be a third tradition descending from Ezra. When we talk about Jews in modern society we nearly always mean those of Jamnia, but we also quite freely use the name, when talking of history, for one or other of the earlier churches. The Zionists, building on this ambiguity, do something a little more complicated: they hold Samaritans, Yemenites and Falashas to be Jews, but Christians not to be. However, the bulk of those supposed to participate as partners in Zionism are in the Jamnia tradition, and some Zionists do use some such narrower definition.

When looking at motives, we must distinguish the motives of those who are Jews within Zionist terminology from those who are not. Among the Jews, there are those who actually believe in Zionism as it is and those who believe in something else which Zionism seems to provide.

1. *Jews* are Zionists either because they are in a hard core(I am not here discussing the strength, only the kind, of their commitment) or because they are tagging along.

1.1 The *Hard Core* has three wings, the vengeful, the nationalist and the Hasidic.

1.1.1 The *Vengeful* are punishing the Palestinians, the first Jewish nation, for acknowledging the false Messiah Jesus of Nazareth,

---

1. Jn 4:9

thus becoming the first Christian nation. When Weiszmann pulled the map of East Africa off the wall in 1903 he was not doing so because the Uasin Gishu was unsuitable for any particular kind of society to develop, nor because he thought of Jews as a nation(he was too learned a Jew for that), but because one particular nation was to be destroyed, even though it had now adopted a third religion. It is for this reason that Zionists count Samaritans as Jews: they too are survivors beyond the Christian treason of the Mosaic tradition. This appears to be the historically central motive for Zionism, those so motivated not being candid about it, although Golda Meir came close to candidness in her historically false but ideologically revealing "There never was a Palestinian people".

1.1.2 *Jewish Nationalists* think of Jews as a nation, despite Nm 23:9 et al. They believe themselves descended from the Jews inhabiting Eretz Israel at the beginning of the Common Era, and claim an inherited right to 'return' thither. George Eliot's Daniel Deronda may have been of this kind. Some who seem to be of this class are just pretending, and really belong to the vengeful class, but do not want to acknowledge that before outsiders whose help they seek—the intelligent will understand.

1.1.3 The *Hasidim* started settlements in Eretz Israel as early as 1777, under Rabbi Menahem Mendel; earlier than the vengeful. The settlement in Eretz Israel is not merely the foundation of a local holy people, like Square Town, for the Square Town Hasidim are usually Zionists as well. The aim is to create a settlement of Jews in Eretz Israel so that the Messiah will be persuaded to come. Other Hasidim with the same intention during Napoleon's march on Moscow had a double pray-in, some praying hard for the victory of each side, so that the mother of all battles would ensue, fulfilling a prophecy, and thus ushering in the Messianic era.

1.2 Some Jews, in a *Penumbra*, support Zionism because it has happened and is somehow associated with them rather than because they believe it should have happened.

1.2.1 *Israeli Patriots* live in Eretz Israel, or remember living there, however they got there, and do not want to lose it. They think opposition to Zionism a threat to their homeland, and the presence of Palestinians a threat to their state, the incorporation of their homeland.

1.2.2 *Pious* people of all faiths tend to dream of an ideal country, or *beulah*, where everyone is of the true faith and lives according to right custom. English Catholics used to idealize southern Europe—where'er a Catholic Sun doth shine—and Carl Sonnenschein built a Catholic village, Marienfelde, in Berlin, for Catholics to go home to after a day's work in that materialist-heretical town. Many people think of the Israeli State as providing such a beulah. Square Town really is one such, and so is the Jewish Quarter of Jerusalem(unless Zionism has undermined that…). As a good land, the Israeli State should be preserved, or at least the Jewish Yishuv or settlement in Eretz Israel should be. It is pleasant but not essential that the land where the faith evolved be a beulah.

1.2.3 Zionism provides a *haven* for Jews persecuted elsewhere, like Kahnawata and Utah for those of other faiths. Kahnawata and Utah were meant as places to build the church up, but served in the meantime as places of refuge. Whether the Jamnia tradition is meant to be built up in Eretz Israel prior to worldwide missionary work I do not know: I have not seen any such plan among Zionists, and Herzl himself, although of this tradition, had no such plans, for he thought of Jews mainly as a nation.

1.2.4 Churches like to have an *ecclesial centre*, something like the Vatican, as a territorial reference point for faith. The Israeli State does not provide this, but it does provide some of the same feelings as go with it. Many Jews think of the Israeli State with the same kind of affection as Catholics used to think of the old Papal States, to save which volunteers from many lands came armed.

1.2.5 *Well-off Jews* do not like poverty-stricken co-religionists in their neighborhoods. As Herzl in *Judenstaat* foretold, French Jews give Jewish immigrants from Eastern Europe a ticket to Tel Aviv rather than help with settling in.

2. *Outsiders* have a variety of reasons, good or bad, for supporting Zionism. There is some parallelism to Jewish reasons, but obviously not, at least among Christians, to that of the vengeful. Some reasons are religious, some secular.

2.1 *Religious* pro-Zionists usually think the Israelis, and Jews of the Diaspora, to be physiologically descended from the Biblical Israelites.

2.1.1 <empty>

2.1.2 *Christian Fundamentalists* think that the Israelis are descendants of the Israelites and therefore worthy of special protection. They even think that God will punish and reward their own countries in accordance with their opposition to or support of Zionism. Many people who are not actually Fundamentalists hold more or less the same doctrines.

2.1.3 *Christian Millenarians,* who are often also Fundamentalists(2.1.2), think that the Israelis are physiologically descended from the Biblical Israelites, and that their successful settlement in Eretz Israel will usher in the Second Coming of the Messiah—with slightly different consequences from those envisaged in Motive 1.1.3.

2.2 *Secular* reasons are very varied. There is often an attempt to justify them on a religious basis.

2.2.1 *Unreflective multinationalists* think Eretz Israel belongs to the Israelis and that anyone wanting to take it from them is a robber. They presume that the world is naturally divided into countries coinciding pretty well to current or recent divisions and that other divisions of the world into countries are artefacts of some wrong.

2.2.2 Those who *confuse church and nation* may think that a church should have a beulah and that the Israeli state constitutes a beulah for Jews.

2.2.3 *Holocaust sympathizers*, obviously erroneously, identify the Israelis, or Jews generally, with those murdered by the Nazis in the ethnic cleansing of Europe from Jews and Gypsies. The Gypsies usually get forgotten. There arises a feeling that to oppose, or even to fail to help, Zionism is to ally oneself with the Nazis and to perpetrate the Holocaust once more. Zionist propaganda regularly makes use of this, trying to identify opponents of Zionism with the Nazis.

2.2.4 Some people think of the Israeli state as something like the *Vatican*, which they think fairly natural to a church. Cardinal O'Connor, Archbishop of New York, expressed such an opinion a few years ago.

2.2.5 *Jew haters* do not want (more)Jews in their countries. The United States seems to have voted in the United Nations for the erection of the Israeli State mainly to stop Eastern European Jews, fearful of a new Holocaust, using New York as their refuge.

2.2.6 *Political cynics* think of the Israeli State as strategically useful for their own purposes. Herzl himself advertised this possibility in *Judenstaat*. A NATO-allied state is seen as a bulwark against

Soviet Communism and Islamic Fundamentalism(Zionist leaders have cultivated both fears), and in general as a strategic base for canal holding and so forth.

2.2.7 *Anti-Arab* people enjoy, for one reason or another, the defeat of Arabs by non-Arabs. The best example of this is those Britons who think of Zionism as their revenge for humiliation by Nasser.

2.2.8 *White Supremacists* think of Jews as their own, perhaps as a slightly inferior branch of their own, and of the Palestinians or Arabs generally as non-White, inferior, worthy of being imperialistically colonized, perhaps even for their own good.

Zionism is thus not a single ideology or ideal but a coincidence of action for several. For this reason it is misleading to talk of "the Zionist mind" and intellectually futile to consider whether Zionism is inherently racialist. There are nearly a score of ideologies or ideals, and the mindset of each must be considered separately, although several(notably 2.2.6 and 2.2.8) may overlap in the same person. To evaluate the arguments of a Zionist, we must first determine which ideal he holds(and which he is pretending to hold); we must also untangle his meanings for the name Israel. We must join the intelligent, who understand.

1995.10.19

Constitutions

CURRENT CONSTITUTIONAL CRISES IN THE WORLD STATE

The English word "state" is from the Latin verb *stare* meaning "stand". The Hebrew word for "state" is *madinah*, from the verb *d[y]n* meaning "judge". A state is thus a standing judgery, as distinct from an *ad hoc* court. Other functions are ancillary or supplementary. The world state was therefore founded in 1899 at the first Den Haag Peace Conference, by the institution of the Permanent Court of Arbitration(PCA), often known as the International Court of Arbitration. The development of the state was delayed(or perhaps accelerated) by its first civil war, the First World War(WW I), after which the organs of the world state were augmented in the League of Nations at the Paris Peace Conference of 1919/1920. A second delay(or acceleration) was the Second World War(WW II), after which the state was subsumed in the United Nations Organization at the San Francisco Conference of 1945. Before discussing the crises which are now being steadfastly ignored let us consider the constitutional history, and first the prehistory, of the world state.

Pre-history

The First World War was not the first world-wide war: some wars we think of as European in scope were actually worldwide because the components of Europe were conquering the world and strove among each other overseas as well as at home. The Napoleonic wars were world-wide. After the final defeat of Napoleon, European states gathered at Vienna in

1815 to regulate or determine their relationships in a "family of nations". A Russian-inspired "Holy Alliance", without organs, of Christian states was formed to bring peace and stability, but this did not cover that broken-away part of Europe called the United States of America, let alone such non-Christian states as the Ottoman, Chinese and Japanese Empires; furthermore, Austria acceded only for an excuse to use its soldiers to suppress liberalism. However, the terms had some influence on political intentions at least until 1899. The Congress of Vienna was succeeded by various tidying-up and extending conferences or congresses culminating in that of Den Haag in 1899, at which, besides Christian states, Turkey, Persia, Siam, Japan and China had joined the "family of nations". This succession of congresses is sometimes called "The Congress System".

It has never come to an end: international conferences of the same general kind are now called every few years by the Economic and Social Council of the United Nations Organization. If our modern conferences seem to do less useful work than those of the Nineteenth Century that is perhaps because the work of the Nineteenth-Century conferences is now done by the General Assembly and the assemblies of the Specialized Agencies of the United Nations: the state has taken over some pre-state functions.

The Nineteenth-Century Congresses included Aachen 1818(evacuation of France), Tropau 1820 and Ljubljana 1821, in both of which Russia pressed for realization of the Holy Alliance, Verona 1822, Paris 1856, Brussels 1874(laws of war), Berlin 1878(cleaning up after the Crimean War), London 1883.

These congresses instituted some permanent international administrative unions, including: the International Telegraph Union(ITU)(Paris 1865)(renamed the International Telecommunications Union in 1934), the International Meteorological Association(1873)(renamed World Meteorological Organization in 1947), the General Postal Union(Bern 1875, with some prehistory in 1863 at Paris)(renamed Universal Postal Union(UPU) in 1878), the International Union for Weights and

Measures(1878), the International Bureau of Health(Washington 1881), the United Central Offices for the Protection of Industrial and Literary Property(Bern 1886), the Bureau for the Publication of Customs Tariffs and for the Abolition of the Slave Trade(Brussels 1890, with opening the next year). These did not constitute organs of a world state, but rather commissions of many states to one(Belgium or Switzerland) to perform quite specific activities, but we can think of them as being informal satellites of the Permanent Court of Arbitration once that was formed, and now, of course, many such unions are Specialized Agencies of the United Nations.

In 1889 the Inter-Parliamentary Union was formed. This took great interest in questions regarding international arbitration, following a line then called "pacifist", rather different from what that word now means.

Den Haag or Arbitration Period

The 1899 Den Haag Peace conference was called by the Czar of All the Russias, still longing for a real Holy Alliance. Like previous congresses, it formulated many treaties and international conventions, mainly about the conduct of war(to effect peace, start by making war more bearable...).

The Permanent Court of Arbitration consists of a set of judges available for international arbitration. When a matter is to be arbitrated, a tribunal is formed from the list, containing one, three or five judges. The general use of the arbitration procedure is for citizens of different states to sue each other but not in each others' home courts. The first case was brought by the United States on behalf of the Catholic Bishops of California against the Mexican government regarding some mission funds the latter held in trust(Mexico paid up). A notable recent tribunal is that judging claims of U.S. and Iranian citizens about property in the other country, agreed to by President Carter and set up in the first days of President Reagan.

Both governments participating have to agree to arbitrate the dispute, as must have been the case between individuals during the early days of human organization. The governments may find it easy to agree because it is very often not government concerns that are at stake. Over the years arrangements have been made for non-governmental entities to submit to arbitration.

To organize things there is as secretariat an International Bureau of the Permanent Court of Arbitration, with an Administrative Council consisting of the ambassadors to the Dutch Crown under the chairmanship of the Dutch Foreign Minister.

The Czar, again, called the 1907 Den Haag Peace Conference(although it was a U.S. idea), which rewrote the Statute of the PCA. It included the Latin American countries, which had not been present in 1899.

The rewritten Statute included amplified provision for International Commissions of Inquiry. Only 5 of these have been held, all between European states about maritime matters. There are also provisions for International Conciliation Courts. Only 3 of these have ever been held.

The Third Den Haag Peace Conference was planned for 1915. We can imagine that there might have been a series of Den Haag Peace Conferences, each called by the Czar, perhaps more than one a decade, until the Conference itself became a permanent organ with a host of satellite organs. Some jurists envisaged such a progress, as did the Interparliamentary Union. But WW I interrupted that, not to mention the Russian Revolutions.

The London Naval Conference of 1909 uttered a Declaration to establish an International Prize Court, attached to the PCA, following an idea discussed in 1907. It was never implemented.

Geneva or League Period

The 1919/1920 Paris Peace Conference had a lot to do. Just as the most important work of the 1899 Den Haag Peace Conference was the PCA, so that of its Paris successor was the League of Nations, via a committee set up for that purpose. Another committee founded the International Labour Organization(ILO), an Affiliated Agency of the League, which continues today as a Specialized Agency of the United Nations. One might have thought that a good location for the League would have been Den Haag, which already had buildings for the PCA, but Geneva was chosen. The League gave the world state an approximately legislative Assembly and an approximately executive Council. In 1921 the Permanent International Court of Justice was formed, with seat at Den Haag, its judges elected from among those of the PCA; it became the supreme judicial organ of the League. It differed from the PCA in that the judges were in office continuously(*permanently*), not merely for one trial at a time.

The United States was very active in various committees and so forth, but did not actually join the League, and that is sometimes said to be the cause of the League's downfall. But in fact the League could not itself wage war, merely arrange some co-operation among its members, and unanimity was required for most purposes in both Assembly and Council. And perhaps there was no downfall: perhaps the League succeeded in many things but just not in one very important one, and the United Nations Organization was a reform of the League as the League was of the PCA system. Successes, perhaps, were the founding of the International Criminal Police Organization(InterPol) in 1923 and the Bank for International Settlements in 1930, but not as a Affiliated Agencies.

The League mandated the administration of certain territories, mainly colonies of the Central Powers(the ones which lost WW I), by states thought competent. The most famous example is Palestine. The most successful is perhaps Papua.

The real reason for the failure to prevent WW II will perhaps best be found in other works of the Paris Conference, notably the Treaty of Versailles.

New York or Organization Period

The 1945 San Francisco Conference founded the United Nations Organization, with seat in New York, as a continuation of the League, and also as a continuation of the victory alliance of WW II(the Soviet Union could not be considered as truly an *ally* of the democracies, so the alliance between "the Allies" and the Soviet Union hight United Nations during WW II). But if the name was taken from the war, the structure was that of the League. The Permanent International Court of Justice was renamed simply "International Court of Justice"(ICJ). The Assembly was called "General" and the Council was replaced by three Councils: Security, Trusteeship(supervising mandates to administer non-self-governing territories) and Economic & Social; but most of the time we hear only of one of them. The need for unanimity was ended, except among the permanent members of the Security Council. One curious difference is that, whereas people were members of the League Council, UN Members are members of the new Councils.

Unlike the League Covenant, the UN Charter has specific chapters about peace-making and -keeping, and provision for armies to come under UN command, as the old pacifists had wanted from the Den Haag Peace Conferences. For this reason the UN has been able to wage war, and so to some extent secure peace, which the League was unable to do. It has been weakened in this regard by the failure to bring to life the Military Staff Committee which the Charter provides for the Security Council.

The UPU, ITU and ILO became, of course, Specialized Agencies of the UN. In 1945 the Food and Agriculture Organization and the

International Monetary Fund were set up; in 1946 the United Nations Educational, Scientific and Cultural Organization(UNESCO), the United Nations International Children's Emergency Fund(UNICEF), and the International Bank for Reconstruction and Development(IBRD, "World Bank"); in 1947 the International Civil Aeronautics Organization; in 1948 the World Health Organization(WHO); in 1956 the International Finance Corporation; in 1958 the Intergovernmental Maritime Consultative Organization(in 1982 renamed International Marine Organization); in 1960 the International Development Association; in 1965 the United Nations Development Program(UNDP); in 1976 the International Fund for Agricultural Development(IFAD); in 1970 the World Intellectual Property Organization; I do not think I have named them all. UN(and related) foundations which have not formally become Specialized Agencies are the International Organization for Standardization(1946), the International Organization for Migration(1954), the International Atomic Energy Agency(1958) and the World Trade Organization(1995). But they are for many practical purposes, not least because of the sharing of members.

Through a variety of activities in the Organization itself and in its Agencies, the UN System is influencing people's lives directly and indirectly. We may disagree about the rightness of a particular influence, just as we may disagree about the rightness of actions of lower-level states. Apart from such differences, though, there are definite crises arising in the UN.

Crises

Orientation

The purpose of every state is to secure such God-given rights as those to life, to liberty and to property. A particular state will inevitably fail, and we may disagree about the best ways of securing rights. What we cannot disagree about is the rule that the state should not itself violate human rights. In fact, however, the United Nations Population Fund Administration(UNPFA), the UNDP, WHO, UNICEF and IBRD are involved in abortion, in cahoots, despite the Universal Declaration of Human Rights and the UN Convention on the Rights of the Child, with the International Planned Parenthood Federation, the most inhuman organization of humans,. The WHO was involved in the testing of the abortifacient drug RU-486. At the International Conference on Better Health for Women and Children through Family Planning in 1987 the following pro-abortion declaration was made: "where legal, good quality abortion services should be made accessible to all women"; this was endorsed by the 5 UN agencies I have just mentioned.

UN family planning concentrates on contraception and abortion, largely ignoring more effective methods such as the Billings Ovulation Method. And, as we can now surely see abundantly, the spread of contraception has caused a great increase in the acceptance of and demand for abortion. The UNPFA statistics show this. This obviously should not be, and when Rep. Christopher Smith tries to hold up UN contributions until sure that they will not be misused in this way he is upholding the very purpose of the UN itself.

There should ideally be no special human-rights agency in any state, because the whole state should be dedicated to the securing of human rights. It has no other purpose. For understandable and legitimate reasons, however, the UN does have a Human Rights Committee. It does not seem to believe in human rights as such, only in the contorted civil rights advanced by such agencies as the ACLU in the U.S. The Committee has rightly condemned police abuse in many lands, but it has also condemned quite legitimate legislation aimed at promoting public health and civic responsibility, such as laws against mutual masturbation. This is a denial of the rights of people living in community to live the most healthy life feasible given the circumstances of the community. Significantly, the Committee has never condemned abortion.

When a suspect is sought on a warrant from a UN court it is quite reasonable that his transport to the court for hearing not be interrupted by local courts. But when a suspect is sought on a warrant from a UN Member he has the right – and, indeed, it is the right of all of us – that he be extradited in proper form, evidence first being shown to an extradition court of the local state in whose territory he is found. On at least two occasions the Security Council has imposed sanctions on "rogue" states for not surrendering suspects without evidence of their guilt.

In these matters we must first, like Christopher Smith, call halt in whatever way we can. But we should also seek constitutional change such that these violations of human rights are unlikely again to be perpetrated by UN organs.

Balance of Power

The League Council had some members appointed by League Members with the permanent power to appoint such members. Similarly, the UN Security Council has five Permanent Members, viz. China, France, Russia, the United Kingdom and the U.S., each with veto power over the Council's actions. The reason for this was originally very practical: these were Members of the UN with real power to sabotage any decision they did not like: they had a real veto power, so they might as well have a legal veto power, thus limiting the scale of planetary civil wars. I imagine that it was fear of a French veto that prevented the UN helping South Vietnam as it had helped South Korea.

We can imagine a different reason for choosing a few such Permanent Members: they might be the nuclei around which we would hope the ideal Members, or at least some ideal Members, of the UN would in the long run form. We might think it obvious that there are too many Members, and, while not being willing and able to do much about it now, choose a few Members which should definitely be there in some ideal future pattern of Members.

Neither France nor the UK fits either of these justifications. Russia also looks rather dubious. Whatever we may think about the veto right at the present stage of evolution of the world state, we have an imbalance.

Protectorates

It has several times happened that the Security Council, in connection with its peace-making activity, has put a country under special protection and direct UN government. This is not provided for in the Charter. That may seem legitimate: the constitution has evolved beyond the constitutional document's provisions. In the U.S. the documentary Constitution reserves to the Congress the right of declaring war, but in fact the U.S. has fought several wars without such a declaration, with only a few people worrying, and usually for the wrong reason(their opinion about the war in question rather than the constitution). A similar evolution in the UN constitution is more serious, however, because the purpose of each protectorate needs to be fitted into a general purpose of all protectorates; we do not know what craziness may in future arise without a framework in the Charter. Furthermore, it would seem that the Trusteeship Council would be a more suitable body than the Security Council to oversee such work.

Unity of Jurisprudence

There is no appeal from a decision of the ICJ. But neither is there appeal from a decision of the PCA. The UN is erecting courts, such as the war-crimes tribunal, which have at best a possibility of reference of points of law to the ICJ, but no right of parties to complain to the ICJ when no such reference is made. This may lead to fragmentation of law, quite apart from the non-state arbitration systems, such as that of the International Chamber of Commerce.

In Germany too there are different hierarchies of courts for: order(civil and criminal), social matters, administration, finance and labor relations. But precisely to prevent fragmentation of the law the supreme courts in these hierarchies have a Common Bench, besides the possibility of appeal, on constitutional issues, to the Federal Constitutional Court. The UN does not have anything similar.

It is unlikely that the UN will in the next few decades evolve any unitary judicial hierarchy: there is going to be specialization of courts for some time to come, probably more than at present. It is important that the various specialisms lead to a common final appeal.

Non-crises

There are several quite serious problems which some people consider constitutional crises but which are really either crises of present policy or long-term problems better considered when the above listed problems are solved.

U.S. Chauvinism

The U.S. has been remarkably chauvinistic about the world state, especially considering the founding principles of the Republic, the motto of the *Liberator*, and the attitude of many people around the world that the UN is a U.S. instrument. Chauvinism elsewhere can often be traced to demagogues trying to keep themselves in power, but in the U.S. we see important legislators who seem more like dupes of demagogues than demagogues themselves. They are to blame(the right word) for the failure of the U.S. to enter the League and for the reservations the U.S. has deposed about the ICJ. They are also in part to blame for recent tardiness in UN contributions.

But that tardiness has other causes. There has, first, been some genuine anxiety about waste in the UN. That is why legislators have been putting riders to appropriations in the attempt to enforce a reform which, apparently unbeknownst to them, has been under weigh for a couple of years, and has been largely implemented. The ignorance of the inappropriateness of this motive is, of course, largely a result of the above-mentioned chauvinism.

A more important cause is a consequence of the Orientation crisis of the UN. The restriction currently proposed by Rep. Christopher Smith would prevent UN-funded family-planning organizations from advocating(let alone paying for or executing) abortion. Congress can in good faith send to the President an apportionment bill that includes abortion restrictions: the UN is able to accept such funds because its financial system is so broken down that a Member of the UN can make its regular contributions for central administration and for peacekeeping without giving any money to UNPFA, let alone the organizations which seem to have UNPFA in thrall. The trouble is that the present President is so rabidly pro-abortion that he only unwillingly signs such bills.

U.S. influence will be undermined if the President continues in his pro-abortion policies. How should Congress relate to the President's surrender of U.S. influence? "To see the raison d'être for the pursuit of power lost in the pursuit of that power renders the whole thing meaningless"(Brian Bethell in *Guardian* 1995.04.21).

When the Orientation crisis of the UN is properly resolved, the chauvinists will find fewer allies in Congress, and it will be clearer how to deal with chauvinism generally. But at present chauvinism as such is less a problem than UN orientation.

Another imbalance

An imbalance of less immediate import than that in the Security Council is that in the General Assembly, where the U.S. and Indian governments, each democratically representing some hundreds of millions of people, each have the same vote as governments with populations four of five orders of magnitude smaller(I do not mention China, because it is very doubtful that its government represents even *one* hundred million people). This is even more absurd than the contrast within the U.S. of Wyoming and California, both having equal representation in the Senate. This imbalance can perhaps be resolved gradually by coalescence of Members. Concurrently, it can some day be resolved by the introduction of democratically elected organs, which might after some decades replace some of the present organs.

Effectiveness

It is often said, especially by those who wish to restrict the UN, that the UN does less than it should. This is partly because of the power structure within it, a separation of powers well constructed at San Francisco. Separation of powers necessarily means that a state will do less good than it otherwise might. It also means that it will do less harm than it might. The unwillingness of Members to supply troops means that aims are not sufficiently shared. The Security Council veto provisions prevent the whole world state falling apart in an attempt opposed by the most power-ful. Both problems can be resolved only by power-separation evolution including democracy, and few people seriously want a democratic world state just yet.

Some ineffectiveness can be countered, especially in military matters, by the proper installation of the Military Staff Committee of the Security Council, and by an extension of the UN civil service tribunal's remit to soldiers under UN command. These are not the most urgent of matters.

Legitimacy

A government is made legitimate by the consent of the governed. The best way to ensure such consent is democracy. But the plethora of ideolo-gies and the lack of orientation of the world state together mean that any attempt at democracy would result in a spatchcock of competing and sometimes conflicting causes, with much chance for entryism by secular inhumanists, enacting things most people did not want. It would be a particularly unsatisfactory democracy. What is more, the few who talk of a world parliament now seem to want something indirect, like the Interparliamentary Conferences, or the European Parliament in its early days. But we know that the European Parliament has continued, even after direct election, in irresponsibility and waste, and the Interparliamentary Conferences too seem to have degenerated. This problem must be carefully tackled in the erection of any democratic structure for the world state. And the Orientation crisis must first be definitely overcome. The lack of legitimacy is therefore a problem for the future, not a crisis of today.

Conclusion

I am not here proposing any solution of the crises, still less submitting a plan for the future constitutional evolution of the world state; I am merely delineating problems. The world state may evolve into a den of unmitigated evil if they are not tackled in the next few years, especially the Orientation crisis. And so may the lower-level states. Muddling through will not suffice.

THE NEXT UN CONSTITUTIONAL CONFERENCE

In 1995 the United Nations Organization was half a century old. Changes to its Charter are being discussed either for the jubilee year(too late now) or for 2000, in what we may as well call the Second San Francisco Conference. Instead of thinking out exactly what the next step in the evolution of the political constitution of the planet should be, the little grey men are talking about trade-offs and fighting for short-term advantage of their own constituencies, here not their countries but the particular social establishments to which they belong. If they were thinking of their countries they would do a lot better, for the benefit of a country is not the same as that of its current rulers, nor even of the influence successions within which themselves not completely selfish rulers are altruist. Yet tabloidal chauvinists of the "countries" will be convinced that their rulers are working for the countries' advantage and actually be inclined to cheer those leaders. The stupid discussions about the permanent membership of the Security Council show this clearly: the probable decision to have 4 European, one almost-European and two other permanent members is the result of jostling by power groups in Britain and France; the inclusion of Japan rather than India comes merely from the lust for prestige.

The little grey men are part of a formidable network of great material, societal and ideological vested interests with corruption at home and aggression(not always physical) against outsiders to cover it up; they love the trickery of tariff and similar juggles, the tyranny of established machines(or of machines they would like to establish); sentiment and patriotism(sometimes called "solidarity") by the bucketful splashing around; dear food for the million, eager labour for the desired structure.

There are other, similar networks—think of those now influencing Christian Aid, the neoprotectionists, the communitarians.

Also in opposition to good governance are secular inhumanists, who will try to prevent the little grey men doing the right things and may persuade them to do some wrong things; with this the tabloidal chauvinists will unwittingly co-operate—or, sometimes, build a case against proper progress by showing how bad wrong progress can be.

All these politicians are afraid that their own favourite schemes will be limited and even that there may be a sea change in human political attitudes, such that they or theirs might later lose power(forgetting, as usual, the purpose for which they have the power). They believe what the *Tao Te Ching* says: dào ke dào fëi cháng dào, i.e. there is no permanent way, no lodestar, we have to play the game one move at a time never looking much ahead and never knowing where we are going or why.

A state is a standing, or permanent, government. The Hebrew word *madinah*, used where English uses *state*, means "judgery". In that sense we have had a world state since 1900, when the Permanent Court of Arbitration was formed. That the Court and its newer co-ordinator, the International Court of Justice, are less used than they might be, that, in fact, the possibility of objective adjudication is often ignored, does not stop us having a state, any more than the Israelites lacked a state in the time of the Judges. Indeed, we are somewhat more developed than that on a world scale, because we have a standing basic arrangement for war, also under-used, whereas the Israelites under the Judges had a more *ad hoc* arrangement. We are in a quasi-Saulide madinah, with unequivocal experience of its inefficacy, and the purpose of the Second San Francisco Conference should be to work us towards a Davidic or Solomonic situation, without the asymmetries which caused the breakdown under Roboam. I may now have exhausted the Israelite analogy.

We have today a variety of courts, mostly hanging on to the ICJ, the latest being the war crimes tribunal, probably soon to be made permanent;

other possibilities come easily to mind. The German Liberals have for decades wanted a Human Rights Court with direct jurisdiction over individuals, perhaps an outgrowth of the UN Human Rights Commission, but this last itself(like the German Liberals as regards human rights at home) needs some straightening out, and such a court would be overwhelmed immediately not only by the number of cases but by the variety of legal and social structures from which they would arise: better start with monitoring of the UN itself and hope for some trickle-down effects while we develop practical methods of actually reaching down.

The purpose of every state is to secure such God-given rights as those to life, to liberty and to property. Around these basic rights we build fences of civil, political, social, economic and cultural rights. Some theoreticians like to talk of protecting and furthering human dignity, with the securing of human rights as central. Plato in the *Laws* was fairly explicit about the details of human dignity, and what he wrote might frighten people: What will happen, they wonder, if the United Nations acts like that? Also, the concept of rights has been degraded by special-interest groups who develop civil and social rights so as to counter the human rights the civil and social rights should be fencing: in the USA, because of an almost accidental and largely irrelevant item in the Bill of Rights, people talk animatedly of a right to bear firearms; the United Nations Human Rights Commission has somehow developed a right to engage in mutual masturbation, and condemned Tasmania for having laws against such misbehaviour, but it does not condemn anyone for abortion: thus do petty-bourgeois concerns distract from the serious work of building a just society(another oft abused term…). Fear for human dignity, as well as the public-health issue, moves many to suspicion of such "rights". The American Civil Liberties Union is pre-eminent in turning people against the idea of rights by emphasizing those of defendants at the seeming expense of the victims of crime, as well as by ludicrous complaints about menorahs in town halls and, worst of all, by advocacy for "abortion rights". When we talk about human rights nowadays we are in danger of quarreling about sometimes minor side-issues while forgetting or even denying the central realities. But the expression "human rights" has not quite yet been put on the scrapyard of fatigued words so deformed by ideological encrustations that they parody themselves in the utterance and must be replaced; let us work against its further belittling.

Although the purpose of states is to secure human rights, it is violation by states that most often impinges on our consciousness: we forget what anarchy might be like and, indeed, those like the Oklahoma City anarchists, "right-wing" anarchists let us say, are particularly vehement in their opposition to evolution of the UN. On the other hand, those who assume the state to be good and the police to be having a hard job get annoyed when they see the police condemned for mistreatment of a prisoner, or a prisoner being let off on "technicalities". Sometimes the technicality is, of course, that he is innocent, but that is not how the press puts it; quite often the police have constructed the technicality by their corruption, but less public anger is directed against them than against the lawyers and judges. ACLU-like groups thus attack reverence for rights partly in good faith as well as in hypocrisy. This is also true of the present UN Human Rights Commission.

Every state should have some assurance that it will not itself violate human rights. The UN is getting influential enough to make this negative principle important and it should be the most important item at Second San Francisco. Indeed, it should be the most important item on the agenda of many constitution-debating bodies at present. How can this assurance be made?

So long as the apparatus developed limits the activity of the Organization, it should not worry xenophobes, chauvinists and sovereigntists. What is required is something that will prevent the United Nations Organization doing wrong without giving it much more direct power to stop the governments of its Members doing wrong(as the USA acquired over its states with the 14th Amendment, for which no general UN equivalent can yet arise). One might argue that the UN is useless if it cannot do that, but it is worse than useless if it itself does wrong, and it has already some powers of compulsion on lower-level political units; a human-rights orientation will not directly increase that and might be seen by many as a welcome limitation. Anyway, decisions of a general-jurisdiction court would be unenforceable unless other constitutional changes were made first, and the Monitor Court proposed below seems good preparation for those changes.

The UN has three major human-rights documents: the Universal Declaration of Human Rights, the International Covenant on Civil and Political Rights, and the International Covenant on Economic, Social and Cultural Rights. The Declaration is meant to be the bedrock on which the other two, and a host of specialized documents, build. Every other document should be building fences around the natural-law principles enunciated in the Declaration. There are some problems with the documents as we have them.

The right to life, in Article 3 of the Declaration, is glossed over, and arbitrarily set to begin at birth, which can be defended only on the assumption that it is a fence around some more basic right(never enunciated) and so not universal, or on the religious doctrine that God breathes in a soul at birth or some other biologically irrelevant time. The C & P Covenant concept of "self-determination of peoples" surely depends on a cyclic definition of "people". Again, there is a very poor basis for property rights. Finally, most economic, social, and cultural rights are aspirations, not strictly rights, so not justiciable. We require a new *Statute of Rights*, with the basic rights to life, liberty and property conceptually central. We should also have explicit the possibility of forfeiting these rights by violating them in others. The civil and political rights should be explicitly referred to the basic rights, as should any of the social, economic and democratic rights included. Because of the strange ways in which people have distorted rights issues, there should be some explicit exclusions of specious rights, such as to masturbation and to suicide. Property rights should be expanded into an outline of rules for protection of real, intellectual and moral property. Language should as far as possible follow that of the present documents to maximize juridical continuity. The specialized conventions on such subjects should probably not get changed at Second San Francisco but rather the offices concerned should be commissioned to restructure their documents later as a matter of lesser importance.

I give a draft of a Statute at Schedule 1. It has as basis the present Declaration, augmented with inspiration from the C & P and ESC Covenants and the U.S. Constitution, and further augmented using ideas from other documents. EuCHR Art. 2 and Mr justice Laws' dictum in *R vs Somerset* (QB 1994) should also be recognizable. There probably needs to be some revision for consistency of language regarding level and obligation of rights, distinguishing, for instance, the perennial right to a fair trial from a consequence in an ordered society, such as the right to counsel, of that right, and both kinds from the right within a developed economy to social welfare protecting the life and liberty of the same person against the slings and arrows of outrageous fortune.

A mere Statute of Rights is not much use, and the Charter itself should be amended to dedicate the Organization to the securing of rights. This dedication should be in Article 1, which needs a new Section 1 for this purpose(Schedule 4). The rest of Article 1 should define Methods(called Purposes in the present text), and Articles 2 and 76(Trusteeship) will also need some adjustment. There should, too, be a practical method of preventing the Organization itself acting against human rights, and the obvious institution is a monitoring court to quash any decision violatory of human rights.

There should be a Human Rights Monitor Court, established in a Protocol to the Statute of Rights, as the European Human Rights Court is by a Protocol to the European Convention on Human Rights, with many benches of first instance, each with three judges. Schedule 2 contains a text for such a Protocol. The judges should not take any cognizance of the suitability of a decision or act for its purpose, merely condemn it to the extent it violates human rights. I am not talking of conforming every decision to the Charter and the Statute in a long-drawn-out procedure, but of a prompt negative correction to conform any decision to the Statute. There is no need for this to be lengthy, as any witness of a German party court knows: such decisions can be made in a matter of hours.

A first-instance bench should attend on each of the General Assembly, the Security Council, the Secretariat and the Economic and Social Council, and on each special Conference. Article 7 of the Charter should thus have a new Section(Schedule 4). In the case of the General Assembly, every Member should have the right to challenge a decision promptly, and to be carefully heard on objective grounds concerning the actual issue. Certain other entities should also have the right of intervention, including a list, to be maintained by the General Assembly, of perhaps 100 NGOs, deletion from the list to require a year's notice. The decisions of these benches should not be "political" in the derogatory sense, as many U.S.(and other) court decisions have alas been, but they should be political in the sense of constantly reiterating the fundamental purpose of political activity.

An appeal bench, of five judges, should sit in Den Haag, with from it appeal to the ICJ of the kind that is possible from other internal UN tribunals(it is not the same kind of appeal as happens in interstate cases). It would be a condition of being a Special Agency that an organization accept the presence and authority of a first-instance bench. One can imagine that intergovernmental organizations such as the OECD and non-governmental organizations such as the ICRC, the IOC and the International Chamber of Commerce would also be willing to accept such monitoring, but the UN could not at this stage in its constitutional development force this. In particular, some courts, such as the European and Inter-American Human Rights Courts, might valuably allow appeal to the Monitor Court.

The monitoring judges would be chosen much as ICJ ones are, but probably for life or on good behaviour, again to be judged much as for the ICJ. The method of choosing judges for the International Court of Arbitration, the ICJ and, in this proposal, the Monitor Court is unsatisfactory but cannot be improved until we have at least one proved chamber of a UN Parliament.

What difference might such benches make? To take a fairly obvious example, the 1994 Cairo Conference on Population would have gone quite differently if every committee preparing its proposed final document had been corrected at every stage by a human-rights bench. Nafis Sadiq was using the conference for an attack on humane principles and an exaltation of secular inhumanism. Had her nastiness been extirpated at early stages the committees would have concentrated on planning good, not evil, and the Holy See would have been spared the tiresome task of buffeting the Conference away from horrors. The final document would perhaps even have been something useful, whereas no progress was made in the whole proceeding to resolution of the problems at issue.

Sticking still with Nafis Sadiq, such a bench attached either to the Secretariat or to the UN Population Fund Administration would undoubtedly veto the funding of abortion, which does now occur. That would have made the UNPFA more humane and so the Cairo conference more valuable.

Another document which would have been vetoed is the Secretary-General's recent edict mandating sex ratios in Secretariat employment. This might in principle be remedied by recourse to the ICJ referring to Articles 8 and 103 of the present Charter, but the people able to take such recourse are for reasons of current ideological fashion unwilling, whereas among the hundred NGOs there would very likely be one moved by different fashion or, we may even hope, one genuinely concerned with human rights.

The present Human Rights Commission, a partial response to calls such as those of the German Liberals for a general human-rights court, exists by virtue of Art. 28-45 of the C & P Covenant. It is probably enough for the Protocol establishing the Monitor Court to refer(Article 21 in Schedule 2) to those Articles, perhaps allowing for later restatement—the ICJ Statute, after all, refers to the 1907 Convention of The Hague.

The bench monitoring the Commission would not have allowed the condemnation of Tasmania for forbidding "homosexuality" because, however unwise such a prohibition may be, no-one's real rights are directly infringed by it. Of course, if Tasmania is punishing same-sex mutual masturbators and not different-sex ones, there might be a case for complaining of inequality before the law, but that was not the issue before the Commission. The Human Rights Commission, although without power, would have more influence for good because it would be condemning violations of genuine human rights, even though its choice of subject might still be tactically dictated. Doubtless movement *against* human rights disguising itself as a movement *for* civil and social rights would be weakened. The same holds for parallel bodies, such as the Committee on the Rights of the Child.

One might argue that there are too many international courts, and that we should be trying to consolidate them rather than to erect new ones, with possible consequences for the unity of law. But there seems no other method than this open at present. General UN courts will not be possible until the UN can directly place obligations on individuals, and that cannot legitimately be done until we have some kind of parliament, something which might be disastrous(v. inf.) without the monitoring I propose.

If one high-level politician puts forward such a scheme at Second San Francisco, using what influence he has to have it properly explained, I believe the change will pass.

The changes here proposed would not worry the tabloidal chauvinists greatly, especially if it were explained that the direct effects would be on the UN and its agencies only, not on "countries". It would arouse the opposition of the secular inhumanists, who would try to bully the little grey men into diluting the Statute, harping on about spurious "rights". The neoprotectionists and communitarians would object to the minimality of the change(which they would say made it almost worthless) and to its emphasis on individual rights(they like social rights, much more fun). But politicians might recognize that the tabloidal chauvinists and most humanly progressive people would support them, the secular inhumanists perhaps not having as many votes as they give the impression of having.

As a logical consequence of a proper Statute of Rights, the United Nations itself should stop its policy of "balance" among Members of its employees. This policy has never been effected, for one reason and another, but it is in the Charter, and should be changed, because, being part of the Charter, the relevant Article will not be automatically changed by the Statute. Furthermore, leaving it as it is might have a kind of contaminating back-up effect on the Statute. The wording in Schedule 3 follows that of the present first sentence of Art. 101(3) and of the 1996 California Civil Rights Initiative, with qualification to allow the suspension of contraction of, for example, military services from an array of thugs, crooks(as the Ukrainians in Yugoslavia) or cowards(as the Indonesians in Cambodia).

Article 8 of the Charter, forbidding sexual discrimination, would thus become superfluous, although it need not be deleted.

Similarly, Article 9 of the Statute of the International Court of Justice ensures that the judges in the Court "represent" the main branches or traditions of law. The proposed Article in Schedule 3 should prevent Buggins rearing his ugly head here.

Let us now consider where the tabloidal chauvinists of Britain and France are most prominently affecting the little grey men. It seems to me obvious that Article 23 should run as in Schedule 5.

The permanent members were originally those with the greatest possibility of *de facto* vetoing a Security Council decision. Obviously Britain and France are no longer in this position and, equally obviously, Europe as a whole is capable of such vetoing if it so chooses. On the other hand, I want the permanent membership to be a foretaste of what the membership of the UN *should* be, and, again, Europe seems a sensible unit into which to divide the world at first cut. The same is true of India taken with some of its smaller neighbours, and India is also a significant military power—more significant than Japan, and more used to UN military work to boot. The promise that Japan will be a candidate at the next redistribution should quieten Japanese chauvinism(though not the outright nutters, just their fellow-travelers), and the other candidatures should also lead to comparative calm at this Conference.

This gives us still a very unsatisfactory composition of the General Assembly, with 'sovereign states' as diverse in significance as San Marino and the PRC. At some time some small states will have to be counted in larger units for UN purposes. The single representation of the WEU in the Security Council and the representation of its member states in the General Assembly may be paralleled after the event of the proposed Art. 23(4), but we can hardly insist on less European representation in the General Assembly when far-off ministates under dubious co-ordination are individually represented. We can hope that in a few decades a UN Parliament will make the Security Council and the General Assembly gradually evolve into a fairly pure head of state, and in the long run the two should be fused, but this is not the occasion for those Charter alterations. There should be no further need to alter Article 23 for a few decades, and by then progress may have been made outside the Charter on these matters.

A Socialist conference in Germany has proposed that the UN Parliament be similar to that with which the European Community started, i.e. having members appointed by the parliaments of UN

Members and without legislative or even scrutiny power. I do not see how this would improve upon the semiannual conferences of the Inter-Parliamentary Union and the annual Commonwealth Parliamentary Conference of the Commonwealth Parliamentary Association. Even giving one of these significant status in the United Nations System would be pointless, as both already have undemocratic member parliaments and either would presumably have even worse ones if it became a UN entity soon. One of the reasons the European Parliament is so irresponsible is its history of powerless and non-representative deliberation. Such a UN Parliament would be even worse than the European Parliament, and once it gained power it might have a tradition of outright nastiness. The UN Parliament, when it starts, must get off on the right foot: it must be directly elected on a constituency basis(with multiple rounds as required), have genuine power of some kind, although very limited at first, and, even more than the European Parliament, have prompt correctives when it gainsays natural rights—and for this we need some such body as the Human Rights Monitor Court. I would like a bench of that Court to look even at committee reports and delete poisonous material, so that proposals against human rights would not come before the plenum for discussion. We should thus have the Monitor Court before we construct the Parliament, so that the latter, although already overdue, must be delayed to a later constitutional convention.

Quite a lot is already doable towards a Davidic or Solomonic situation by the Special Agencies(the WTO will be doing a great deal; fortunately its prehistory largely constrains it to good) and such non-UN bodies as the BIS and the OECD, but these do not require UN Charter change, and the proper co-ordination of such work must await a democratically elected UN Executive, something further away even than a Parliament. For some time to come the Administrative Committee on Co-ordination, led by the Secretary-General, is the best we can have.

There are proposals around for many other changes in the Charter, but most of them would require a Parliament for democratic legitimacy. Even of those that would not, many would be pointless without co-operation among Members that is possible under the present Charter but not forthcoming—notably the failure to use the Military Staff Committee as now defined(Art. 46), and to keep troops in reserve for UN use, as the Charter "requires". Perhaps a separate conference could consider a set of agreements under Art. 43(we are still using the transitional provision of Art. 106). To achieve these improvements, changes in the Charter would be useless as the immediate progress required is outside the wording of the Charter, and the same holds for compulsory ICJ jurisdiction as might be introduced by a change in Art. 36(3). The same externality is true of the composition of the General Assembly: evolution of UN Members actual and ideal is not a Charter matter, even though it constrains Charter evolution. I opine therefore that the above changes to the Charter are the only ones which should emerge from Second San Francisco.

1996.01.15

revised   1997.05.04

Schedule 1

TEXT OF STATUTE OF RIGHTS

Whereas the reasons for making the Universal Declaration of Human Rights still hold,

Whereas the Declaration and its dependent documents have proved of value in advancing the cause of Human Rights,

Whereas, however, error and malice have distorted rights issues and thus misled many, to human detriment, even on the supposed basis of the Declaration, so that a Restatement has become necessary,

Now, therefore,

THE UNITED NATIONS

proclaims this

STATUTE OF RIGHTS

as its own binding orienting leitmotif and a common standard of achievement for all peoples and polities.

1. All persons are free and equal in dignity and rights, which derive in the first place from their sophont potential for reason and conscience, which obligates them to act towards one another in a spirit of brotherhood; the specific biological nature of the somatic generation of *Homo sapiens* determines them in more detail. Rights of other kinds of organisms are different insofar as they are biologically different and lesser insofar as they are essentially incapable of reasoning.

2. Everyone is entitled to all the rights and freedoms set forth in this Statute without distinction based on race, color, sex, language, religion, political or other opinion, ethnic or social origin, property, birth, status of polity of citizenship, or other personal status.

3. Everyone has the right to life, liberty and security of person and property. All other rights are consequences or corollaries of, or fences around, these basic rights. They may be forfeited only by violating them.

4(1). Everyone has duties to the community, in which alone the free and full development of his personality is possible.

(2). In the exercise of his rights and freedoms, everyone shall be subject only to such limitations as are determined by law solely for the purpose of securing due recognition and respect for the rights and freedoms of others and of meeting the just requirements of morality, public order and the general welfare in a democratic society.

(3). These rights and freedoms may in no case be exercised contrary to the same rights in others.

(4). No state, group, or person may engage in any activity or perform any act aimed at the destruction of the rights and freedoms recognized in this Statute or at their greater limitation than is provided for in this Statute.

5(1). A public agency has no rights of its own which it enjoys for its own sake; all its dealings constitute the fulfilment of duties which it owes to others, and it exists for no other purpose.

(2). Nothing in this Statute implies for any polity, group or person any right to engage in any activity or to perform any act aimed at the destruction of the rights and freedoms set forth herein.

(3). Each party to this Statute undertakes to respect and to ensure to all within its territory and subject to its jurisdiction the rights proclaimed in this Statute.

(4). Each State party to this Statute undertakes:

(a) to ensure that any person whose rights and freedoms herein proclaimed are violated shall have effective remedy, especially if the violator acts in an official capacity;

(b) to ensure that any person claiming such a remedy shall have his right thereto determined by competent authority within its legal system, and to develop the possibilities of judicial remedy;

(c) to ensure that competent authorities enforce such remedies.

(5). There shall be no restriction upon or derogation from any of the human rights recognized or existing in any state pursuant to law, convention, regulation or custom on the pretext that this Statute does not recognize a right or recognizes it to a lesser extent, but no right exists to violate a right recognized in this Statute.

6(1). In time of officially proclaimed public emergency threatening the life of society states may derogate from their obligations under this Statute as strictly required in the situation.

(2). Such derogation shall not conflict with other obligations under international law, nor allow discrimination by race, color, sex, language, religion or social origin.

(3). No derogation from Articles 7, 8(1), 9, 11, 14(4), 18 or 25 may be made.

(4). Any state party to this Statute shall immediately inform the Secretary-General of the United Nations of the derogated provisions and reasons for the derogation. It shall make a further communication on termination of the derogation.

7(1). Everyone has the inherent right to life. This right shall be protected by law. No-one shall be arbitrarily deprived of life.

(2). Sentence of death may be imposed only for the most serious violations of human rights in accordance with the law in force at the time of the violation, such law not being contrary to the provisions of this Statute.

(3). Apart legitimate hangwite in case of grave government incapacity, sentence of death may be executed only when uttered by a court following conviction of a crime for which this penalty is provided by law and after an opportunity for appeal against the conviction and the sentence and to seek pardon or commutation of the sentence.

(4). Sentence of death shall not be imposed for crimes committed by those under 18 years of age, or on pregnant persons.

(5). Deprivation of life shall not be regarded as in contravention of this Article when it results from the use of force which is no more than absolutely necessary:

  a. in defence of any person from unlawful violence;

  b. in order to effect a lawful arrest or to prevent the escape of a person lawfully detained;

  c. in action lawfully taken for the purpose of opposing a riot, insurrection, invasion or other belligerent attack.

(6). Nothing in this Article shall be invoked to delay or prevent abolition or restriction of capital punishment by any polity.

(7). A right to suicide is not found in this Statute.

8(1). Everyone has a right to recognition everywhere as a person before the law.

(2). Everyone has the right to liberty and security of person.

9(1). No-one shall be held in slavery or servitude, except in punishment of crime; slavery and the slave trade shall be prohibited in all their forms.

(2). Compulsory military or alternative service, service exacted in emergency or calamity threatening the life or well-being of the community, and normal civil obligations do not constitute slavery or servitude.

10. No-one shall be subjected to arbitrary arrest, detention or exile.

11(1). No-one shall be subject to torture or to cruel, inhuman or degrading treatment or punishment.

(2). No-one shall be subjected without his free consent to medical or scientific experimentation.

12(1). No-one shall be subjected to arbitrary interference with his privacy, family, home or correspondence, nor to attacks upon his honor or reputation.

(2). Warrants shall not issue for searches and seizures but upon probable cause, supported by oath or affirmation, and particularly describing the place to be searched and the person or thing to be seized.

(3). No soldier shall, in time of peace, be quartered in any house, without the consent of the owner, nor in time of war but in a manner prescribed by law.

(4). Everyone has the right to the protection of the law against such interference or attacks.

13(1). Everyone has the right to freedom of movement and residence within the borders of each state.

(2). Everyone has the right to leave any country, including his own, and to return to his country.

(3). The above-mentioned rights shall not be subject to any restrictions except those which are provided by law, are necessary to protect public security, order, health or morals, or the rights and freedoms of others, and are consistent with the rest of this Statute.

(4). No-one shall be arbitrarily deprived of the right to enter his own country.

(5). An alien lawfully in a territory may be expelled therefrom only in pursuance of a decision reached in accordance with law and shall be allowed to submit the reasons against his expulsion and to have his case reviewed by, and be represented for the purpose before, the competent authority or persons designated by the competent authority.

14(1). Anyone arrested shall be informed at the time of his arrest of the reasons for the arrest and of any charges against him.

(2). Anyone arrested or detained shall be brought promptly before a judge or officer authorized to act as a judge and shall be entitled to prompt release or trial within a reasonable time. It shall not be the general rule that persons awaiting trial be detained in custody, but release may be subject to guarantees to appear for trial and related judicial proceedings.

(3). Anyone arrested or detained shall be entitled to take proceedings before a court for decision without delay on the lawfulness of the detention and for order of release if the detention is not lawful.

(4). No-one shall be imprisoned merely for inability to fulfil a contractual obligation.

(5). Any victim of false arrest and unlawful detention shall have an enforceable right to compensation.

(6). Persons deprived of their liberty shall be treated with respect for the inherent dignity of the human person.

(7). Accused persons shall, except in exceptional circumstances, be segregated from convicted persons and shall be subject to separate treatment appropriate to their status as unconvicted persons.

(8). Accused children shall be separated from adults and be brought with most rapidity to adjudication.

(9). The penitentiary system may never impose more than a just punishment. Besides appropriate punishment, it should aim at the reformation and social rehabilitation of the offender. Children shall be segregated from adults and accorded treatment appropriate to their age and status.

(10). Everyone convicted of a crime shall have the right to review by a higher tribunal of his conviction and sentence.

(11). A person who has suffered punishment by reason of miscarriage of justice has the right to compensation as declared in Article 5(4).

(12). No-one shall be liable to be tried or punished again for an offence for which he has already been finally convicted or acquitted in accordance with applicable law and procedure.

15(1). Everyone has the right to own property alone as well as in association with others.

(2). Everyone has the right to fair wages and equal remuneration for equal work.

(3). Everyone has the right to the protection of the moral and material interests resulting from any scientific, literary or artistic production of which he is the author.

(4). No-one shall be arbitrarily deprived of his property.

(5). No law shall impair the obligation of legitimate contracts.

(6). Property rights are not absolute. Ownership obliges.

(7). Private property shall not be taken for public use without due compensation.

(8). A right to possess weapons or poisons contrary to public welfare and without due countervailing cause is not found in this Statute.

(9). A people may not be deprived of its own means of subsistence.

(10). A right to potlatch is not found in this Statute.

16(1). All are equal before the law and are entitled without any discrimination to equal protection of the law. All are entitled to equal protection against any discrimination in violation of this Statute and against any incitement to such discrimination.

(2). Everyone has the right to an effective remedy by competent tribunals for acts violating rights granted or guaranteed by constitution or other applicable law.

(3). Everyone is entitled in full equality to a fair and public hearing by an independent and impartial tribunal in the determination of his rights and obligations and of any criminal charge against him.

(4). The press and public may be excluded from part of a trial only for reasons of morals, public order or security of a democratic polity, when the interests of the private lives of the parties so require, or when strictly necessary in special circumstances where publicity would prejudice the interests of justice.

17(1). Everyone charged with a criminal offence shall have the right to be presumed innocent until legally proved guilty.

(2). In the determination of any criminal charge, the accused shall be informed promptly in a language which he understands of the nature and the cause of the charge against him.

(3). An accused shall have adequate time and facilities for preparation of his defence, including counsel of his own choosing.

(4). Trial of criminal charges shall take place without undue delay.

(5). An accused has the right to be tried in his presence and to defend himself in person or by legal assistance of his own choosing; to be informed of this right if he does not know it; to have legal assistance assigned to him when justice so requires, and without payment if he lacks sufficient funds to pay for it.

(6). An accused has the right to examine or have examined the witnesses against him and to obtain the attendance of witnesses on his behalf under the same conditions as witnesses against him.

(7). An accused has the right to the free assistance of an interpreter if he cannot understand or speak the language used in the court.

(8). No-one may be compelled to testify against himself except concerning his actions committed under color of law and public office claimed by the testifier and recognized by the court as legitimate.

(9). Procedures against juveniles shall be such as to take account of their age and the special desirability of their rehabilitation.

18(1). No-one shall be held guilty of any criminal offence consisting of an act or omission not a criminal offence when committed, nor shall a heavier penalty be applied than the one applicable at the time of the crime.

(2). This Article does not impede the trial and punishment for any act or omission which, at the time it was committed, was criminal according to the general principles of law recognized by the community of nations.

19(1). Everyone has the right to seek and to find in other places, including where appropriate other countries, asylum from persecution.

(2). This right may not be invoked in the case of prosecutions genuinely arising from non-political crimes or from acts contrary to the Methods and Principles of the United Nations.

20(1). Everyone has the right to citizenship.

(2). No-one shall be arbitrarily deprived of citizenship or denied the right to change citizenship.

21(1). Unmarried men and women of marriageable age have, without any limitation due to race, nationality or religion, the right to marry and found a family.

(2). Marriage can be contracted only with the free and full consent of both intending spouses.

(3). Men and women have equal rights to marry, in marriage, and at suspension or dissolution of marriage.

(4). At marriage each spouse grants the other lifelong exclusivity of sexual access.

(5). A right to masturbation, whether solitary, concerted, or mutual, is not found in this Statute.

22(1). The family is the natural and fundamental group unit of society and is entitled to protection by society and the State.

(2). States parties to this Statute shall take appropriate steps to ensure equality of rights and responsibilities of spouses before, during and after marriage. In the case of suspension or dissolution, provision must be made for the necessary protection of the children.

(3). Motherhood and childhood are entitled to special care and assistance.

(4). Special protection, including paid leave or leave with adequate social security benefits, should be accorded to mothers during a reasonable period before and after childbirth.

23(1). Every child has, without discrimination as to race, color, sex, language, religion, national or social origin, property or birth or conception whether in or out of wedlock, the right to such measures of protection as are required by his status as a minor, on the part of his family, society and the State.

(2). Every child shall be registered immediately after birth and shall have a name.

(3). Every child has the right to citizenship.

(4). Employment of children in work harmful to their morals or health, or dangerous to their life or likely to hamper normal development, should be punishable by law.

24(1). Everyone has the right to freedom of opinion.

(2). Everyone has the right to freedom of expression, including the freedom to seek, receive and impart information and ideas of all kinds, regardless of frontiers, orally, in writing including print, in a form of art, or through any media of his choice.

(3). The exercise of the rights listed in Section 2, carrying with it special duties and responsibilities, may be subject to restrictions, but only such as are provided by law and are necessary:

(a) for respect of the rights or the reputation of others;

(b) for the protection of national security or of public order, or of public health and morals;

(c) to prohibit propaganda for war;

(d) to prevent advocacy of sectional hatred constituting incitement to unjust discrimination, hostility or violence.

25(1). Everyone has the right to freedom of thought, conscience and religion.

(2). This freedom includes that to adopt a religion or belief of his choice and, either alone or in community, in public or in private, to manifest his religion or belief in worship, observance, practice or teaching.

(3). No-one shall be subject to coercion which would impair his freedom to choose or change his religion or belief.

(4). Freedom to manifest one's religion or beliefs may be subject only to such limitations as are prescribed by law and are necessary to protect public safety, order, health, or morals or the fundamental rights and freedoms of others.

(5). Parents and, where applicable, legal guardians shall have the liberty to ensure the religious and moral education of their children in conformity with their own convictions.

(6). Satanism, that is, the service of an opponent of a God held by the server to be the source of good, in rebellion against such a God, cannot be held to be in accord with anyone's conscience, and therefore no-one has the right to practise it.

26(1). Everyone has the right to freedom of peaceful assembly.

(2). No restrictions on this right may be imposed except in conformity with law and as necessary in a democratic society for national security, public safety, public order, protection of public health or morals or the protection of the rights and freedoms of others.

27(1). Everyone has the right to freedom of peaceful association with others, including the right to form and join trade unions for the protection of his interests.

(2). Restrictions of this right may by law be placed on members of the armed forces and of the police.

(3). Other restrictions on this right may be imposed only by law and when necessary in a democratic society in the interests of national security or public safety, public order, the protection of public health or morals or the protection of the rights and freedoms of others.

(4). Trade unions have the right to function freely subject only to the restrictions of Sections 2 and 3.

(5). Trade unions may establish federations and confederations at national and international level.

(6). There exists a right to strike.

(7). No-one may be compelled to belong to an organization.

28(1). Every citizen has the right and shall have the opportunity to take part in the conduct of public affairs, directly or through freely chosen representatives.

(2). Every citizen shall have the right and opportunity to vote and be elected at genuine periodic elections which shall be by universal and equal suffrage and shall be held by secret ballot, guaranteeing the free expression of the will of the electors, which will shall be the basis of the authority of government.

(3). Every citizen shall have the right of access to public service.

(4). When a political unit is divided into lower-level political units, each of those units at the first level down should have an equal right of economic, social and cultural self-determination. Formal exceptions should be grounded in genuine difference of the distinguished lower-level unit, such as physical isolation from the others, or presence of common cultural, material or physical features, distinguishing it from the others taken together.

29(1). Everyone, as a member of society, has the right to social security and is entitled to realization, through national effort and international co-operation and in accordance with the organization and resources of each state, of the economic, social and cultural rights indispensable for his dignity and the free development of his personality.

(2). Everyone has the right to a standard of living adequate for the health and well-being of himself and of his family, including food, clothing, housing, medical care and necessary social services, and to security in the event of unemployment, sickness, disability, widowhood, old age or other lack of livelihood outside his control.

30(1). Everyone has the right to the opportunity to gain his living by work which he freely chooses or accepts and by purchase of goods and services of quality and price he chooses.

(2). The states parties to this Statute undertake to realize this right by technical and vocational guidance and training and policies to achieve full and productive employment under conditions safeguarding the individual's political and economic freedoms.

31. Everyone has the right to just conditions of work, namely

a. safe and healthy working conditions;

b. equal opportunity subject to seniority and competence to promotion at work;

c. rest, leisure, reasonable limitation of working hours,

periodic paid vacations and remuneration for public holidays.

32(1). Everyone has the right to education. It should be free, at least in the elementary and fundamental stages. Elementary education should be compulsory. Technical and professional education should be generally available and higher education should be equally available to all on the basis of merit.

(2). Education should be directed to the full development of the human personality and to the strengthening of respect for human rights and fundamental freedoms. It should promote understanding, tolerance and friendship among all nations, races and religious groups; it should further the activities of the United Nations for the maintenance of peace.

(3). Parents have a prior right to choose the kind of education that shall be given to their children.

(4). Individuals and bodies are free to establish and direct educational institutions subject to the principles in §§ 1 and 2 and to minimum standards set by the state.

33(1). Everyone has the right freely to participate in the cultural life of the community, to enjoy the arts and to share in scientific advancement and its benefits.

(2). Persons belonging to ethnic, religious or linguistic minorities shall not be denied the right, in community with the other members of their group, to enjoy their own culture and to use their own language.

34. Everyone is entitled to a social and international order in which the rights and freedoms set forth in this Statute can be fully realized.

35. This Statute supersedes the Universal Declaration of Human Rights and the International Covenant on Civil and Political Rights. Other human-rights documents of the United Nations remain in force, except where they contradict this Statute, until appropriately rescinded.

36(1). States may accede to this Statute by deposit with the Secretary General of instruments of accession.

(2). The Secretary General of the united Nations shall inform all Members of the United Nations and any other States which have acceded to it of the deposit of each instrument of accession.

37. For each State acceding to it, this Statute shall enter into force three months after the deposit of its instrument of accession.

38. The provisions of this Statute extend to all parts of federal states without exception.

Schedule 2

TEXT OF PROTOCOL TO STATUTE OF RIGHTS

1. The United Nations Human Rights Monitor Court shall be constituted and shall function in accordance with the provisions of this Protocol.

2(1). The Court shall be composed of independent judges chosen regardless of citizenship or ethnicity from among persons skilled in natural and positive law and dedicated to human rights on a basis of natural law as expounded in the Statute of Rights.

(2). The President of the International Court of Justice shall be Rector of the Human Rights Monitor Court.

3. The Court shall have Local Benches, each of three judges, monitoring particular entities, and an Appeal Bench, of five judges.

4. The judges shall be elected in accordance with Articles 4 through 12 except 10(3) of the Statute of the International Court of Justice; but notice under Article 5(1) shall be at least 1 week and no more than 6 weeks, except for the first election.

5. Elections for the Appeal Bench shall be distinguished from those for Local Benches. Judges who have served on a Local Bench shall be considered by nominators at elections for the Appeal Bench.

6(1). Judges serve for life.

(2). The resignation of a judge shall be addressed to the Rector for transmission to the Secretary-General, upon which the judgeship becomes vacant.

(3). Judges shall continue to discharge their duties until their places have been filled, and even then shall finish any cases which they may have begun.

7(1). No judge may exercise any political or administrative function, or engage in any other occupation of a professional nature.

(2). Any doubt on this point shall be settled by a decision of the International Court of Justice.

(3). Notwithstanding Section 1, a judge continues as a member of the Monitor Court after election as a member of the International Court of justice, but may not function as a judge in the Monitor Court while a member of the International Court of Justice.

8. No judge may act as agent, counsel or advocate in any case.

9(1). No judge may be dismissed unless, in the opinion of all or all but one of the members of the International Court of Justice, he has ceased to fulfil the required conditions.

(2). The International Court of Justice may consider such an opinion on its own initiative or at the request of any of the following: the Appeal Bench of the Monitor Court, two thirds of the judges of the Monitor Court, any of the principal organs of the United Nations, or any Special Agency of the United Nations.

(3). Formal Notice thereof shall be made to the Secretary-General of the United Nations by the Registrar of the International Court of Justice.

(4). This notification makes the place vacant.

10. Articles 19, 20 and 23(Sections 2 and 3) of the Statute of the International Court of Justice apply *mutatis mutandis*.

11. A Chairman of the Appeal Bench and sufficient chairmen for the Local Benches shall be elected in accordance with Article 4.

12(1). The Rector shall appoint judges to the Local Benches, allocating to each a chairman who, when possible, shall be of those so elected under Article 11.

(2). In appointing judges to the Local Benches, the Rector shall provide that every entity to be monitored always have a complete Local Bench actually available.

13. The Registrar of the International Court of Justice shall act as Registrar to the Appeal Bench.

14(1). The clerical facilities of the International Court of Justice shall be available to the Appeal Bench.

(2). The clerical facilities of the entities monitored shall be available to the Local Benches.

15(1). If a judge considers that he should not take part in a decision of his Bench, he shall so inform the Rector.

(2). If the Chairman of the Appeal Bench, the Chairman of the Bench to make a decision, or a majority of the Appeal Bench or of a Bench to make a decision, considers that a judge should not take part in a decision of that judge's Bench, they shall so inform the judge and the Rector.

(3). If the Rector considers that a judge should not take part in a decision of that judge's Bench, he shall so inform the judge and the Chairman of the Bench in question. In the case of an information as in Section 2, he shall be held so to consider until he pronounces on the question.

(4). If the Rector or a judge considers that the judge should not take part in a decision, the judge shall be replaced by another judge of the Court for that decision, unless no judge is easily available before the lapse since notification of the case of six hours for a Local Bench or one week for the Appeal Bench, when the judge shall despite the consideration take part in the decision.

(5). In case of disagreement on this issue by the judge and the Rector, or of agreement contrary to an information as in Section 2, the question shall be decided by the International Court of

Justice, whose decision shall not affect the validity of a decision made in either event of Section 4.

16. Citizenship, nationality and race of a judge do not affect suitability to hear any case.

17. Each Bench shall sit with a full complement of judges.

18(1). Each judge shall receive a salary.

(2). Chairmen, and judges of the Appeal Bench, shall receive special allowances.

(3). Judges acting at the Rector's appointment as Chairman or on the Appeal Bench shall receive special allowances while they so act.

(4). These salaries and allowances shall be fixed by the General Assembly. They shall not be decreased during office.

(5). Regulations made by the General Assembly shall fix the conditions of retirement pensions and traveling expenses for judges.

19(1). The expenses of the Rector and of the Appeal Bench shall be borne as part of those of the International Court of Justice.

(2). The expenses of the Local Benches shall be borne by the entities monitored.

20(1). Each Local Bench is open to the entities it monitors, to the Secretary-General, to Members of the United Nations and members of the Security Council, to states deliberating in the entity monitored, and to other authorized intervenors.

(2). It is also open to voting members of the entities monitored and to recognized participants in international conferences monitored.

(3). In the event of dispute the initial decision as to open-ness shall be made by the Local Bench. The Rector shall make rules for appeal against such decision, the ultimate decision to be made by the International Court of Justice.

21(1). The Committee established in Articles 28-45 of the International Covenant on Civil and Political Rights continues in life and function, henceforth to uphold the Statute of Rights rather than the Covenant.

(2). A Local Bench monitors the Committee.

(3). Any natural or juridical person affected by a solution or other human-rights decision uttered by the Committee is an authorized intervenor. No-one is held to be affected by an utterance of the Committee merely because it refuses to condemn a law which might be used against him.

22(1). Every permanent observer of the General Assembly recognized as a central reference of a major faith community is an authorized intervenor.

(2). The General Assembly shall authorize as many as 100 non-governmental organizations as intervenors in the Local Benches monitoring the principal organs of the United Nations, taking due account of the variety of interests of such intervenors.

(3). The General Assembly may deauthorize as intervenor any organization authorized in accordance with Section 2, giving two years notice.

23. The Economic and Social Council shall specify for each international conference and each organization referenced in Article 63 of the Charter what intervenors shall be authorized in the Local Bench monitoring it.

24. The Appeal Bench is open as regards any matter decided by a Local Bench to the parties in the Local Bench on that matter, to parties which could have been present, to the Secretary-General, to Members of the United Nations and to the intervenors of Article 22.

25(1). The purpose of the Court is to forbid violation of human rights by the entities monitored and to quash spurious condemnations on grounds of human rights by them, particularly by the United Nations Human Rights Committee.

(2). It shall apply natural law, principally as expounded and developed in the Statute of Rights.

(3). It shall not judge the suitability of a measure within an actual context for its alleged purpose, nor the real purpose of the authors, but only the conformity of the measure to human rights.

(4). It shall not judge the conformity of a measure to applicable positive law except where such conformity is directly necessary to secure human rights.

26(1). Each Local Bench shall proceed and deliberate in any language it holds suitable.

(2). Decisions and judgements of a Local Bench shall be written in English or French for transmission to the Appeal Bench.

(3). The Appeal Bench shall proceed and deliberate in English, French or the language used in the Local Bench, as the Appeal Bench holds suitable.

(4). Decisions and judgements of the Appeal Bench shall be written in English or French for transmission to the International Court of Justice.

27(1). A case is brought before a Local Bench by notification by one of the authorized intervenors within a reasonable time of the decision it is sought to gainsay. If a consequence of a decision is not immediately obvious, notification may reasonably be made within a reasonable time of the consequence becoming clear. The notification need not be in writing.

(2). A case is brought before the Appeal Bench by written notification within a week of the final decision of a Local Bench.

(3). The Bench shall promptly ensure that all authorized intervenors are made aware of the notification and proceed at once with whatever can be dealt with at once, including at least a preliminary statement of the case.

28. The Bench shall have the power provisionally to forbid any execution of the decision under scrutiny.

29. Intervenors may have the assistance of agents, counsel or advocates promptly introduced.

30(1). The entity monitored shall provide at request of the Bench all information it may have which the Bench may need, unless the Bench judges it better that an intervenor or, in the case of the Appeal Bench, the Registrar obtain such information.

(2). The entity monitored shall provide any clerk needed to take minutes and otherwise attend on the Bench as instructed by the Chairman. Only minutes signed by the Chairman are authentic.

31. The hearing shall be under the control of the Chairman.

32. The hearing shall be in the presence of any authorized intervenor desiring to be present, and of the general public as convenient.

33. The Bench shall call the intervenors present for their arguments as soon as the intervenors are available, allowing due delay when argument depends on some person or thing not actually present.

34. Articles 54 through 57 of the Statute of the International Court of Justice apply *mutatis mutandis*.

35. The judgement shall be signed by the Chairman and read in public, preferably, when a Local Bench is deciding, before the entity monitored. It shall state what parts of the decision scrutinized are stricken.

36. The judgement has immediate effect on the decision scrutinized, but a judgement may continue the suspension of an approved decision during appeal or revision.

37. A decision by the monitored entity not to consider a new fact, or to construe its importance as an intervenor thinks unfit, may justify a new notification under Article 27(1).

38(1). An application for revision of a judgement may be made if the intervenor seeking the revision indicates specifically where the argument of the judgement may be mistaken.

(2). Proceedings for revision shall be essentially as for an original case, but focused on the alleged mistake.

(3). Refusal to make a revision makes a judgement final.

39(1). Appeal from the judgement of a Local Bench is made as under Article 27(2).

(2). Appeal from the judgement of the Appeal Bench is by advisory opinion of the International Court of Justice, sought by the Appeal Bench or other body authorized in accordance with Article 65 of the Statute of the International Court of Justice.

Schedule 3

CHANGES TO CONFORM THE CHARTER TO THE STATUTE OF RIGHTS

101(3). The paramount consideration in the employment of the staff and in the determination of the conditions of service shall be the securing of the highest standards of efficiency, competence and integrity. Neither the Organization nor any of its agencies shall use race, sex, color, ethnicity, national origin or citizenship as a criterion for either discriminating against or granting preferential treatment to any individual or group in the operation of the Organization's systems of employment, contracting or services. This Article does not prevent the temporary exclusion of use of services of a particular kind from a political unit whose services are shown to be ineffective for the purposes of the Organization.

.

.

.

ICJ Statute

9. At every election, the electors shall bear in mind not only that the persons to be elected should individually possess the qualifications required, including an appreciation of the diversity of legal traditions, but also that in the body as a whole there should be a good understanding of the total juridical heritage of humanity.

Schedule 4

CHARTER CHANGES TO ORIENT THE UN TO THE STATUTE OF RIGHTS

1(1). The Purpose of the United Nations is to protect and enhance human dignity by securing to all such human rights as those to life, to liberty and to property, as defined and fenced in the Statute of Rights annexed to and an integral part of this Charter; the Statute binds the Organization.

(2). The Methods of the United Nations are:

1. To achieve international co-operation in promoting and encouraging explicit and implicit respect for human rights as set forth in the annexed Statute of Rights, so solving international problems of an economic, social, cultural or humanitarian character;

2. To maintain international peace and security, and to that end: to take effective collective measures for the prevention and removal of threats to the peace, and for the suppression of acts of aggression or other breaches of the peace, and to bring about by peaceful means, and in conformity with the principles of justice and international law, adjustment or settlement of international disputes or situations which might lead to a breach of the peace;

3. To develop friendly relations among nations based on respect for the principle of equal rights and self-determination of peoples, and to take other appropriate measures to strengthen universal peace; and

4. To be a centre for harmonizing the actions of polities in the execution of these common ends.

2. The Organization and its Members, in pursuit of the Purpose stated in Article 1, using the Methods also therein stated, shall act in accordance with the following Principles:

1. The Organization shall itself never violate human rights, nor induce or encourage others to do so.

2. All Members of the Organization enjoy sovereign equality.

3. All Members, in order to ensure to all of them the rights and benefits resulting from membership, shall fulfil in good faith the obligations assumed by them in accordance with the present Charter.

4. All Members shall settle their international disputes by peaceful means in such manner that international peace and security, and justice, are not endangered.

5. All Members shall refrain in their international relations from the threat or use of force against the territorial integrity or political independence of any state, or in any other matter inconsistent with the Purpose or methods of the United Nations.

6. All Members shall give the United Nations every assistance in any action it takes in accordance with the present Charter, and shall refrain from giving assistance to any state against which the United Nations is taking preventive or enforcement action.

7. The Organization shall ensure that states which are not Members of the United Nations act in accordance with these Principles so far as may be necessary for the maintenance of international peace and security.

8. Nothing contained in the present Charter shall authorize the United Nations to intervene in matters which are essentially within the domestic jurisdiction of any state or shall require the Members to submit such matters to settlement under the present Charter; but this Principle shall not prejudice the application of enforcement measures under Chapter VII.

.

.

.

7(3). To each principal organ, except the International Court of Justice, and to subsidiary organs as designated by the General Assembly, is attached a bench of the Human Rights Monitor Court established in the Protocol to the Statute of Rights, available at all times to monitor its activities at appropriate request and to veto those contrary to human rights.

.

.

.

62(4). It may call, in accordance with the rules prescribed by the United Nations, international conferences on matters falling within its competence. To each such conference, including its preparatory committees, shall be assigned a bench of the Human Rights Monitor Court.

63(1). The Economic and Social Council may enter into agreements with any of the agencies referred to in Article 57, defining the terms on which the Agency concerned shall be brought into relationship with the United Nations. Such agreements must include attendance on the Agency of at least one bench of the Human Rights Monitor Court. The agreements shall be subject to approval by the General Assembly.

(2). It may co-ordinate the activities of the specialized agencies through consultation with and recommendations to such agencies and through recommendations to the General Assembly and to the Members of the United Nations.

(3). The Economic and Social Council may enter into agreements with other intergovernmental and worldwide economic and social organizations whereby those organizations accept monitoring at their own expense by a bench of the Human Rights Monitor Court.

.

.

.

76. The basic objectives of the trusteeship system, in accordance with the Purpose and Methods of the United Nations laid down in Article 1 of the present Charter, shall be:

a. to encourage respect for human rights and for fundamental freedoms for all without distinction as to race, sex, language or religion, and to encourage recognition of the interdependence of the peoples of the world;

b. to further international peace and security;

c. to promote the political, economic, social and educational advancement of the inhabitants of trust territories, and their progressive development towards self-government or independence as may be appropriate to the particular circumstances of each territory and its peoples and the freely expressed wishes of the peoples concerned, and as may be provided by the terms of each trusteeship agreement; and

d. to ensure equal treatment in social, economic and commercial matters for all Members of the United Nations and their nationals, and also equal treatment for the latter in the administration of justice, without prejudice to the attainment of the foregoing objectives and subject to the provisions of Article 80.

Schedule 5

CHARTER ARTICLES ON COMPOSITION OF THE SECURITY COUNCIL

23(1). The Security Council shall consist of fifteen members. China, the Western European Union, Russia, the United States of America and India shall be permanent members of the Security Council. The General Assembly shall elect as non-permanent members of the Security Council ten Members of the United Nations not included in the permanent members of the Security Council, due regard being specially paid, in the first instance to the contribution of Members to the maintenance of international peace and security and to the other purposes of the Organization, and also to equitable geographical distribution.

(2). The non-permanent members of the Security Council shall be elected for a term of two years. In the first election of non-permanent members after the inclusion of the Western European Union and India among the permanent members, as many non-permanent members shall be elected for a period of one year as shall be required to ensure that half the non-permanent members be replaced each year.

(3). Each member of the Security Council shall have one representative.

(4). When Russia becomes part of the Western European Union a majority of the General Assembly shall choose to replace it as permanent member of the Security Council one of the following: the East African Common Services Organization, South Africa, the Economic Community of West African States, Brazil, the Arab League, the Organization for Economic Co-operation,

Japan, the Association of South East Asian Nations, Australia. Sentence 2 of Section 2 applies *mutatis mutandis*.

.

.

.

86(1). The Trusteeship Council shall consist of:

a. the permanent members of the Security Council;

b. all Members of the Organization, other than permanent members of the Security Council, administering trust territories;

c. as many other Members elected for three-year terms by the General Assembly as may be necessary to ensure that the total number of members of the Trusteeship Council is equally divided between those which administer trust territories and those which do not.

Schedule 6

SOURCES OF STATUTE ARTICLES

Statute	UDHR	C & P	ESC	US Constitution other
1	1			
2	2		2(2)	
3	3			D of I §2 s.1 Rand:
				Virtue
				ch.12 §10
				GGfdBRD
				Art.2(1),18
4(1)	29(1)			
(2)	(2)		4	
(3)	29(3)			
	30			
(4)		5(1)	5(1)	
5(1)				A10 QB 1994 R vs
				Somerset
(2)	30	5(2)	5(4)	
(3)		2(1)	1(3)	
(4)		2(3)		
(5)		5(2)	A9	
6(1)		4(1)		
(2)		(1)		
(3)		(2)		
(4)		4(3)		
7(1)	3	6(1)		
(2)		(2)		
(3)		(2)		
		(4)		

		14(5)	
(4)		6(5)	
(5)			
			EuCHR Art.2
(6)		6(6)	
(7)			res nova
8(1)	6	16	
(2)	3		
9(1)	4	8(1)	A13
		(2)	
		(3)a	
		b	
		c(i)	
(2)		(ii)	
		(iii)	
		(iv)	
10	9	9(1)	I 9 §2
11(1)	5	7	
(2)		7	
12(1)	12		
(2)			A4
(3)			A3
(4)			A4
13(1)	13(1)	12(1)	
13(2)	13(2)	(2)	
(3)		(3)	
(4)		(4)	
(5)		13	
14(1)		9(2)	
(2)		(3)	
(3)		(4)	
(4)		11	

(5)	9(5)		
(6)		10(1)	
(7)		(2)a	
(8)		b	
(9)		(3)	A8
(10)		14(5)	
(11)		(6)	
(12)		(7)	A5
15(1)		17(1)	
(2)		7a(i)	
(3)		27(2)	I 8 §8
(4)	17(2)		
(5)			I 10 §1
(6)			GGfdBRD Art.14(2)
(7)			A5
(8)			A2
(9)	1(2)	1(2)	
(10)			res nova
16(1)	7		
(2)	8		
(3)	10	14(1)	
(4)		(1)	
17(1)	11(1)	14(2)	
(2)	(3)a		A6
(3)	(3)b		
(4)	(3)c		
(5)	(3)d		
(6)	(3)e		A6
(7)	(3)f		
(8)	(3)g		A5
(9)	(4)		

18(1)	11(2)	15(1)		I 9 §3
(2)		(2)		
19(1)	14(1)			
(2)	(2)			
20(1)	15(1)			
(2)	(2)			
21(1)	16(1)			CJC c.1058
(2)	16(2)	23(3)	10 n.1	CJC c.1057
(3)		23(2)		
(4)				CJC c.1055 §1
				1056
21(5)				res nova
22(1)	16(3)	23(1)		
(2)		23(4)		
(3)	25(2)			
22(4)			10 n.2	
23(1)		24(1)		
(2)		(2)		
(3)		(3)		
(4)			10 n.3	
24(1)	19	19(1)		
(2)	19	(2)	A1	
(3)		(3)		
(3)a		(3)a		
(3)b		(3)b		
(3)c		20(1)		
(3)d		20(2)		
25(1)	18	18(1)	A1	

(2)	18	18(1)		
(3)		(2)		
(4)		(3)		
(5)		(4)		
(6)				res nova
26(1)	20(1)	21		A1
(2)		21		
27(1)	20(1)	22(1)	8(1)a	
		23		
(2)		22(2)	8(2)	
(3)		(2)		
(4)			8(1)c	
(5)			b	
(6)			d	
(7)	20			
28(1)	21(1)	25a		
(2)	(3)	b		D of I §2 s.2
(3)	(2)	c		
(4)		1(1)	1(1)	I 9 §6
29(1)	22			
(2)	23(2)			
	25(1)			
30(1)	23(1)		6(1)	
	(3)			
(2)	(2)			
31			7	
a			b	
b	23(2)		c	
c	24		d	
32(1)	26(1)		13(1)	
			(2)	
(2)	(2)			

PROPOSED AMENDMENT TO THE TREATY OF MAASTRICHT

The Treaty on European Union shall be amended in accordance with the following provisions.

1. In Article F:

    —the following Section shall be inserted:

    "1. The objectives of the Union and of the European Community, and the purposes of the Union and of the European Community, set out in Article B and elsewhere, are within the general purpose of all polities, viz. the protection and furthering of human dignity mainly by the securing of such God-given rights as those to life, to liberty and to property.";

    —the following Section shall be inserted:

    "3. The Union does not limit the securing of human rights by a Member State, which may therefore forbid

        (a) the violation of the human rights of its citizens and residents in the territory of a sister state,

        (b) the violation by its citizens and residents of human rights in the territory of a sister state,

        (c) travel by its citizens or residents to the territory of a sister state there to violate human rights

    and

132

(d) the incitement of its citizens and residents to the violation of human rights in the territory of a sister state even when the sister state does not itself currently forbid the violation.";

—the present Section 3 shall become Section 4;

—the present Section 1 shall be superseded by the following Sections:

"5. The powers not delegated to the Union by this Treaty or by the Member States are reserved to the Member States or to the people.

6. The union may fix the rate or amount of a tax levied by a Member State only to fix the common external tariff, to feed some common fund of the Union(and then only to the extent that the tax flows thereto) or to impose strictly hypothecated internalization of an economic cost.".

2. In Article L:

—the following point shall be inserted:

"(b) Articles F and K.2;";

—the present point (b) shall become (c);

—the present point (c) shall become (d).

3. The Declaration of Guimaraes interpreting Protocol 17 to the Treaty on European Union is repealed as superseded; the Protocol is repealed as redundant.

1995.01.10

Note: Protocoll 17 and the Declaration of Guimaraes are fudges about abortion.1997.05.13

LEGISLATION AGAINST TERRORISM

to: the Right Honourable Lord Lloyd of Berwick, Chairman
    Inquiry into Legislation against Terrorism
from: John A. Wills

Terrorism is a word invented to describe the government of one period of the First French Republic; it indicates government by intimidation directed by the party in power, as distinct from the element of intimidation essential to all government when that intimidation is directed according to the rule of law. Subjection to the laws is not the same as subjection to the legislature or any part of the government. More generally, terrorism is policy intended to terrify those against whom it is directed, because the rule of law is in some way ineffective. Notably, the rule of law may be ineffective because it does not provide for change, or because its procedures do not allow the change wanted by the party engaging in terrorism.

As an example, the Fourth French Republic's skyjacking(the first skyjacking) of a plane with Algerian rebels among its passengers resulted from inability to capture those people through ordinary extradition procedures and the intention to deny those people the change they sought(alteration of state boundaries) through the ordinary political process.

For another example, the IRA engages in terrorism to compel change(again, of state boundaries) not achievable through the actual democratic process precisely because the change desired is a change in the democratic structure(a change in the units within which democratic decisions would be made).

Una buena parte de esta violencia deriva de una ficción política, de la idea de que a través de un sistema y un conjunto sistemático de ideas se puede capturar la realidad en su totalidad y expresarla, organizarla y reformarla de manera perfectamente lógica. Cada ideología conduce en última instancia al fanatismo y el fanatismo no es más que una ficción que trata de imponerse como una realidad en nombre de la ciencia.

Maria Vargas Llosa on *Mayta*
in January 1986
cit. NYT 2 Feb. 1986
AP 2 Feb. 1986
La Opinión 3 Feb. 1986

Any legislature concerned with the suppression of terrorism must as its highest priority ensure that the state of whose structures it is part not itself engage in terrorism. More generally, the legislature should ensure that its state is executing the common purpose of all states, viz. the securing of the basic human rights to life, liberty and property; the first step in reformation of any state is ensuring that the state itself not violate those rights. There is little point in state action against private-enterprise mass-kidnapping if the state itself is imprisoning hundreds of innocent people, falling into the error of which Llosa warns. The state's own system and conjunction of ideas must always refer back to its own purpose.

As regards the UK, it must first be ensured that every government officer is civilly liable for misconduct in office. This was meant to be the consequence of the Actions Against the Crown Act of a few decades ago, but there has been some back-sliding, which should be corrected. Next, relations with foreign states should take this into account. The United States does not allow civil suit of criminal prosecutors for malicious prosecution, even when the grossest frame-ups have occurred(cf. *Imbler vs Pachtman*), and extradition to the United States should always be conditional on the renunciation of this anomalous right by any prosecutor involved in the case, until the anomaly is removed from U.S. law.

Similarly, the UK must not be a harbour for those who want to violate human rights better protected in their own countries. The UK has chosen(mistakenly in my opinion, but that is another matter) not to protect the right to life of preborn children, for which reason some people journey to the UK to frustrate the somewhat more protective laws of their own country. Abortion at least should become illegal when it would be illegal in the usual residence of the child and mother. This does not of itself mean that abortion should be universally illegal in the UK, merely that the UK should not frustrate the attempts of sister states to do better than the UK in some respects.

The following principles should be thoroughly incorporated into UK law:

1. All persons are free and equal in dignity and rights, which derive in the first place from their sophont potential for reason and conscience, which obligates them to act towards one another in a spirit of brotherhood; the specific biological nature of the somatic generation of *Homo sapiens* determines them in more detail. Rights of other kinds of organisms are different insofar as they are biologically different and lesser insofar as they are essentially incapable of reasoning.

2. Everyone has the right to life, liberty and security of person and property. All other rights are consequences or corollaries of, or fences around, these basic rights. They may be forfeited only by violating them.

3. A public agency has no rights of its own which it enjoys for its own sake; all its dealings constitute the fulfilment of duties which it owes to others, and it exists for no other purpose.

The best way to do this is probably a *Statue of Orientation* containing the above principles, introduced by Act of Parliament, declaring the Queen's purpose to be to secure to all within her power such God-given rights as those to life, to liberty and to property, forfeited only by those violating them in others. All law is to be interpreted as in some way the fulfilment of this purpose. Let any extant law not so interpretable be to that extent repealed in the Act introducing the Statute, preferably explicitly, where present law allows the Queen's servants to violate human rights(e.g., the NHS doing abortions, Scots courts jailing arrested people for a fortnight without even hearing a plea, courts everywhere granting no-fault divorces without joint consent), by minimum amendment of extant statutes; in a blanket fashion where no-one has noticed the incompatibility of a law with human rights.

For practical implementation the Statute itself should explicitly forbid any servant of the Queen to claim that the Queen ordered him to violate any human right, and allow remedy by civil suit and appropriate orders(notably mandamus) to prevent any government officer violating human rights. The possibility of criminal-law remedy should not be covered in this Statute, although perhaps the Introductory Act might make a few provisions for specific violations.

The difficulty of having a Bill of Rights and continuing parliamentary sovereignty can be resolved fairly easily: Parliament would be free to pass future laws violating human rights, but the Human Rights Committee of each House on observing such a Bill before its House would have the obligation to lay before Parliament minimum amendment to conform the Bill to the Statute. This obligation of the Committee would be enforceable by mandamus. I do not think such a limitation of the freedom of a Committee would worry those genuinely concerned with the principle of Parliamentary sovereignty, although it might worry those actually concerned with something else.

The state itself not violating its own purpose, how can it best hinder others from terrorism? The fanaticism decried by Llosa is often the motive for terrorism, and we must ensure, so far as in us lies, that the terrorism we oppose is illegitimate. It might be legitimate as rebellion or as hangwite.

Rebellion against a democratic government is always illegitimate(I do not mean one may not legitimately rebel against a democratic state for extension of democracy to a territory not covered by the state's democracy, such as a colony). To prevent legitimate rebellion, the whole world must become democratic. How to evolve the world as a whole towards democracy is not something we can propose as legislation, but the U.S. has shown that starving dictatorships in America of weaponry transforms them into democracies. It took about a decade, and the same effect in Araby, say, would doubtless take longer, especially as the UK is a proportionately smaller supplier there than the U.S. in America, but the way is clear: no arms export license should issue except for a democratic purchasing government. Other qualifications should be considered only after this hurdle has been jumped. The UK will thus cease to encourage most illegitimate terrorism. There is a good chance that the UK example would be followed by some other arms-exporting states, but even if not the UK should have such a restriction on its arms sales.

So far as I know, the only legitimate hangwite in the UK would be the killing of abortionists, which does not in fact occur. For purity of intention, however, the UK, besides the NHS no longer doing abortions, should step by step limit the legal impunity of this wrong.

Neither directly nor indirectly encouraging terrorism, how can the state oppose that which nevertheless arises? By two methods: intelligence and police. These overlap somewhat, but my suggestions for legislation are distinct.

Everyone should be given the background intelligence to understand that the precise delimitation of a political boundary is a far less important matter than the effectiveness of the political units on the sides of the boundary and of the political unit encompassing both. Somehow language classes in schools should emphasize this. It is fairly obvious to me, and presumably my English Language textbook(Ronald Ridout: *English*

Today) helped me with the analysis. Legislation regarding the national curriculum should mandate that Key Stage 4, at latest, should give the pupil a sense for false argument based on improper collective substantives. The tremendous courage shown by some terrorists might then be directed to nobler aims.

M.I.5, instead of, or perhaps as well as, helping the police, should edit an annual *Review of Radicals*. This should describe all known organizations and movements for radical change in society. Not only the IRA, but International Planned Parenthood Federation, Hizb ut Tahrir, Society for the Protection of the Unborn Child and the Better World Society should be described in it. Inclusion should not be by known danger but by radicalism, recognizing that fanaticism may be around the corner if great frustration sets in. The Review should describe: any organizational structure(difficult in this Age of Aquarius), including the links of such organization sets as SF/IRA, IPPF/FPA; attitude towards basic human rights, e.g. IPPF opposed, IRA contemptuous, SPUC affirmative, etc.; attitude towards use of extant structures to effect new ones; history of violence. Interested parties should have the right by mandamus to correct errors for future editions. This document would be of value for all interested in the smorgasbord of ideas about changing the world, and in particular for popular and police understanding of politically motivated violence.

Anyone who has been bethieved knows that the police have very little concern for finding the thief and the stolen goods. They register thefts as losses, when they think they can get away with it, to keep the figures low, and bribe prisoners to submit false "take into consideration" and other secondary statements to keep the "solved" rate as high as they can.

How to improve enthusiasm I am not sure. Enthusiasm is certainly important: after a single nasty murder the police very often find the culprit, admittedly with extraordinary effort, while the IRA weapons bunkers in Kerry and some other county are still unlocated, even with 18 months of ceasefire, surely of some value for the detection.

To speed criminal procedure, arrested people should be taken promptly for arraignment, even at night: there should always be a magistrate on duty. This would mean faster conviction of the guilty and less opportunity for the police to frame the innocent. It would also lessen resentment at mistaken false arrest, and so lessen support for unconstitutional methods of change.

Submitting a "t.i.c." or other secondary confession should automatically trigger information of the victim and encouragement to demand compensation. That should reduce the false incidence, and perhaps increase real detection rates. Terrorists would suffer along with other criminals.

The method of late appeal from criminal sentence, as when police corruption is later detected, should no longer be via the Home Secretary but by petition to the trial court for examination of new evidence and rehearing of the disputed point. To this end, the prosecutor should at trial submit detailed proposed Findings, as in civil cases, for the jury to consider. This improved and more objective appeal facility should discourage future wrongs as were done to the Birmingham Six, and the police would be more encouraged to find the real terrorists.

By observing strict justice one can decrease support for illegitimate movements, even when many people think the aims of the movement right. When causes of resentment are addressed justly, as for example in the Northern Ireland procedure of strictly ignoring irrelevant details of an applicant for a public post, terrorist groups are gradually starved of support. Once the Statute of Orientation is in force its negative effects may by default have positive results such as to reduce the frustration at failure to implement some ideal system.

There is little in this submission of exclusive application to terrorism. That is because terrorism is a means, not an end, or even a class of end, and because acts of terrorism are crimes independently of their inclusion in a terrorist program. The important thing in combating terrorism is to ensure that the state itself not become terrorist, for then it has no purpose in combating terrorism.

1996.02.27

Note: I translate Llosa's explanation thus:

A good part of this violence derives from a political fiction, from the idea that via a system and a systematic conjunction of ideas one can capture reality in its totality and express, organize and reform it in a perfectly logical manner. Every ideology leads in last instance to fanaticism and fanaticism is no more than a fiction which tries to impose itself as a reality in the name of science.

1997.05.15

PROPOSED AMENDMENT TO THE CONSTITUTION OF THE UNITED STATES

1. We hold these truths to be self-evident: that all men are endowed by their Creator with certain unalienable rights; that among these are those to life, liberty and the pursuit of happiness; that governments are established to secure such rights, holding their just powers from the consent of the governed.

2. The expression "all men" in the preceding Section covers all individuals of sophont generations of biological species, notably of the somatic generation of *Homo sapiens*.

3. An unalienable right may be forfeited by violation of the rights of others or by threat of such violation; in a state of government such forfeited rights may be restored by law.

4. The pursuit of happiness consists centrally in the holding of property.

5. The purpose of government being to secure rights, government may never violate rights; when agents of government violate rights the victim always has the right to redress in civil law.

6. All human, civil, political, social, economic and democratic rights secured by or defined in this Constitution, or in the laws, are to be understood as derivative from the central principle stated in the first Section of this Article.

1995.06.16

Proposals

THE DIRTY QUERY

About 1920 Mukkistan was partitioned into two new states, Filthistan and Dirtistan. The partition was largely the result of long-standing agitation by Dirty Nationalists, who did not, however, get precisely the partition they had wanted: they wanted their bright new Dirtistan to include the city of Gongslow and its environs, but this area became part of Filthistan.

Dirtistan immediately fell into civil war between those who wanted immediate war against Filthistan for the 'recovery' of Greater Gongslow for 'Whole Dirtistan' and those who hoped to consolidate the Dirty state for a while and then somehow wheedle Greater Gongslow out of Filthistan. Both sides in this civil war alleged that Whole Dirtistan, to which no state for over a century had corresponded, rather than Mukkistan, had been partitioned.

Filthistan had inherited Shittipore, long the capital of Mukkistan, and even used the old Mukki administrative and cultic buildings. By some oddity it also inherited the old Mukki army, including regiments primarily recruited in areas now assigned to Dirtistan(the Ndevu Ndogo, sovereign of both states, is said to have wept, in his Filthy capacity, or perhaps in memory of lost Mukkistan, at the suspension of four such regiments), and the bulk of the Mukki state debt(to the relief of investors, who would have been unable to collect much from Dirtistan during its civil war), but it refused to assume responsibility for certain bonds issued explicitly for the compulsory purchase for landless peasantry of farmlands now within Dirtistan. Dirty Panjandrums, by some constitutional oddity entitled to appear for the rest of their lives in the Panjambund of the Filthy Majlis, complained bitterly about this for some years, but to no effect.

The ancient Beestly Hinaraj, entirely surrounded by Mukkistan, and now stuck between the two new states, remained independent, and its 70-year-old special relationship with Mukkistan, a relationship thought by many Mukkis to be centuries old, was transformed into a similar relationship with Filthistan.

So far as I can determine, Beest has never been claimed as part of Whole Dirtistan. This is curious, because the term *Dirty* was originally synonymous with *Straitbeit*, and Beest is historically more Straitbeit than some places which *are* claimed for Whole Dirtistan. There are also regions of Filthistan beyond Gongslow with much stronger Straitbeit-language traditions than Greater Gongslow but which Dirty nationalism does not claim.

The inhabitants of Greater Gongslow belong for the most part to the Shite sect, while the majority of Dirties are Turd. Since partition, the Turd proportion in Greater Gongslow has increased, certain erotic activities tending to depress the birthrate being less clearly condemned by the Shite than by the Turd clergy. Oddly, such behaviour has also become popular in Dirtistan, especially among the laxist-tending Turds of Harfing, the capital(founded long ago by invading Stationfolk, whose chain of ministates also included Beest). Shites in Greater Gongslow often accuse Turds, whom they not very accurately identify with dreamers of the Whole Dirtistan myth, of being irresponsible, bigotted and judgemental in their rejection of non-sexual eroticism. Traditional Shites furth of Greater Gongslow tend to condemn such practices even more harshly than Turds, although for different theological reasons.

In Greater Gongslow the majority even of Turds wish the partition line between the Mukki states to remain unaltered, but the Shites are even more adamant. Originally they objected to the idea of partition at all, although they are now so accustomed to it that they become embarrassed if one broaches the subject of re-uniting Mukkistan by dissolving the border completely. Dirty nationalists, once they realise that the proposal is actual ending of partition rather than the repartitioning they call 'ending the partition of Whole Dirtistan', go into fits of rage at such a suggestion, raving of Filthy imperialism and Mukki colonialism and anachronistic policies. There is most definitely a Whole Dirtistan and, most strongly in Greater Gongslow, a Whole Filthistan tendency, but the Whole Mukkistan beloved in centuries past by those who never saw it is not consciously sought to any significant extent. It does, however, still exist, as you will find out pretty quickly if you tell almost any Dirty that Ingoutbad, say, is the most beautiful city in Filthistan: they claim Harfing is, because they identify lost Mukkistan, to which they instinctively feel they belong, with extant Filthistan, which they condemn as oppressive and alien. Recently some newspapers even claimed, to giggles rather than outrage, that the Dirty Republic(which has succeeded the raj of the Dirtily advised Ndevu Ndogo) was the only part of Filthistan represented in the International Dung-Scattering Contest. I will return to this aspect of the problem.

The Shites of Greater Gongslow think of themselves as specially pleasing to God due to their love of civil and religious liberties, to preserve which they have consistently prevented Turds achieving power over Shites. The Gongslow *Shite Intelligencer* once had an approving historical article on Shallspud Apl's work to secure religious freedom and to that end wisely disallowing Turdery. The Gongslow Shite sees Greater Gongslow as in the forefront of Shitery and the attendant liberties; he has a confused image of Greater Gongslow as a place of refuge for Shites subject to persecution(although none has ever fled thither), like Kahnawata or Nagasaki; as a place of consolidation from which to spread Shitery to the world(although Shite mission work from Greater Gongslow is minuscule), like Utah; as a place of holiness in which the good may in comfort approach the numinous, like Square Town; as a centre for faith-based answers to religious and moral questions(although no Shite elsewhere pays much attention to the decisions of Greater Gongslow synods), like the Vatican. God has somehow given Greater Gongslow to the Shites for all these purposes, and any non-Shite tolerated in the territory must recognise the magnanimity of the Shites in allowing his continued presence in the shadow of Shitery, like a non-Jew in Gush Emunim's Eretz Israel or a non-Muslim in Hamas's Waqf Falastin or Palestine Glebe.

Curiously enough, some Dirty nationalists have a similar vision, one somewhat nearer to reality: Greater Gongslow Turds do sometimes flee to Dirtistan; Dirty missionaries are quite a significant force in worldwide Turdery. The Turd Gross Mufti does not, of course, reside in Dirtistan, so the Dirty Turd does not have that kind of dream. Abwert, the first Dirty President, who had been influential in the mayhem and murder leading to the partition of Mukkistan, declared on the radio one Acharya Pleb that he had always wanted to make Dirtistan 'the home of a people who valued material wealth only as the basis of right living and devoted their leisure to things of the spirit'.

These dreams, not wholly opposed to each other, really have very little to do with political structures at all, let alone political boundaries. Both Filthistan and Dirtistan have by and large freedom of religion, and both Turd and Shite believe the numinous related to individuals regardless of which side of a political boundary they live on. Both communities are free to build physical and social structures in either state for the fulfilment of their dreams of one or other holy land, and moving the border will not affect these rights. Indeed, the quarrel over the border, due to its linkage in the minds of many to religious questions, is a hindrance to serious consideration of the claims of the two faiths.

The Turd muftis of Filthistan, in which the majority of the people are neither Shite nor Turd but Edgite, find the association of Turdery with Dirty nationalism a distraction from their presentation of their religion to post-Edgites otherwise ready for conversion. The consequences for Shitery are even worse: once when I was abroad—not far, oddly enough, from the academy at which Shallspud Apl did his military training—a friend sent me the *Shite Intelligencer* with a letter starting 'Please find enclosed a copy of the best Turd propaganda available in Plasticome'; but it is far more harm to Shitery than help to Turdery. There is no real hope for any co-operation between Shite and Turd, for their ideas are quite different, but both should be more afraid of intuitionism than of each other, and it is precisely certain kinds of intuitionism that the identification with partition-related opinions helps, for it is to such forms of (ir)religion that the post-Edgite is most inclined. Questions of the right treatment of religious groups are really quite distinct from border questions.

The feeling of persecution among Turds in Greater Gongslow is also best tackled independently of border questions. Wherever borders may run, action affirmative of particular religious ratios in employment is wrong. The purpose of all states is to secure such human rights as those to life, to liberty and to property, and if either Dirtistan or Filthistan is failing in this task it should reform itself accordingly. It seems to be true that Dirtistan at present secures the basic rights better than Filthistan, although those who survive may end up better off in Filthistan than in Dirtistan. For both aspects the present situation of each state should be examined and plans made for transformation. In most of Filthistan, for instance, parents may under quite a wide range of circumstances have their children put to death, either privately or by public executioner. This is not permissible in Dirtistan, and one might argue that transfer of any part of Filthistan to Dirtistan would improve the world human-rights situation—but the rectification of Filthy law would still be the duty of us all, and in any case Filthy law is so asymmetric that practically no murder is permissible in Greater Gongslow, and even illegal murders are rarer there than in some other parts of Filthistan.

There still remains the question of the border between Filthistan and Dirtistan. Although not so important as made out, this problem does require a solution. The Filthy government insists that the question should be answered by the people of Greater Gongslow. Silent Kraut, the leading Dirty nationalist in Greater Gongslow, says this is wrong, Greater Gongslow being a completely artificial unit, and that the question should be put to the people of Whole Dirtistan. As a matter of fact, Greater Gongslow was more carefully crafted(at the time of the Partition of Mukkistan) than the one-time Whole Dirtistan which Silent Kraut thinks so obvious and natural—an *ad hoc* creation, I suspect, by Cockrein the Fat to contain Turd resistance to his efforts to establish Edgery throughout non-Shite areas of Mukkistan. I may be wrong, but in any case if we agree that Whole Dirtistan is the natural unit to which to pose questions we have no need to ask it *whether* it should be such a unit. Similarly, if we assume, with the Filthy government and most civic leaders in Greater Gongslow, that Greater Gongslow is a natural political unit there is no need to ask whether it should irrevocably sink into Whole Dirtistan because we have already decided it should not.

The bounds of a political unit cannot be determined(except under the mongrel creed of 'might makes right') by the unit itself. To suggest that they can is to talk nonsense. Even if the Dirty government had the power and the will to conquer Greater Gongslow it would undoubtedly allege some kind of justification perceived to be valid at a higher level. The question is how humanity should subdivide itself politically. It is as human beings that we should make this decision, not as Dirties, or Filthies, or Mukkis. We might in our first ideal division of the world place all this disputed territory in Goodspart(both Filthistan and Dirtistan do in fact belong to the Goodspartic Association) and then we would have to decide, within a Goodspartic context, as citizens of an ideal Goodspart, how Goodspart should be subdivided. The claim that Harfing is the most beautiful city in Filthistan may be one clue as to the most natural division, but the arguments should all be Goodspartic and in principle valid for all Goodspart, not merely for solution of the Dirty Query. Our logically prior subdivision of the world, *a fortiori*, should be on human or Terran bases valid for the whole planet, not just for any Goodspart we might think a suitable unit. Whether a rational subdivision of Goodspart would lead to units closely similar to Mukkistan, Filthistan, Beest, Dirtistan or Greater Gongslow I do not say, but political self-definition is just a very dangerous kind of question-begging.

1995.08.04

A SINGLE CURRENCY

Europe is struggling in its attempt at having a single currency, mainly waffling about harmonization and convergence, whereas the monetary authorities of the whole world should be working towards a single currency for the whole planet. The wanton loss of commercial power bewailed by Ruskin somewhere in *Munera Pulveris* ch. II is still with us, nowadays often taking the form of large-scale crises with severe loss of savings and aggravated poverty, 95 years after the institution of the world state in the initial shape of the Permanent Court of Arbitration(if you doubt that that gives us a state, meditate on the Semitic word *madinah*) and half as long since the inauguration of the macroeconomic authority of that state—and for what? So that local politicians can devalue to "restore lost competitiveness" without addressing the causes(usually themselves) of the loss; so that they can induce spurious feel-good factors just in time for elections; so, sometimes, that they can boast how strong their currency is relative to that of other countries. Pretty poor reasons.

The U.S. Federal Reserve System(Federal Reserve Board with many Federal Reserve Banks), stripped of its regulatory functions, seems an excellent model and even nucleus for a planetary currency authority. The short-term aspects of non-monetary politics hardly affect it, due to a clever constitution; it need heed no arbitrary political boundary; its local governors are appointed for reasons other than party membership.

The US$ is already used quite a bit outside the US for many transactions, despite the declining centrality of the US$ to exchange rates. This makes less of a difficulty than some other expanding currency area would have.

Thanks to Hollywood the world dreams itself U.S.American, so this idea should arouse much less ire than the Euro project has done. Only politicians would object, for much the same reasons as they have fouled up the Euro process, and anti-Yankee politically-minded people, who should at least be pleased that a UN special agency would be the reference "government". I think(I hope) we can forget the neoprotectionists.

The IMF Board of Governors would be the legislator for an International Reserve Board, but only Governors for countries already using the UN$ or whose currency authorities already had integration agreements and were on time with all implementation of those agreements should have votes on IRB matters.

At world level, bank-regulatory functions are performed by the Bank for International Settlements, and are quite separate from IMF work for the most part.

The US$, like any currency, has its strength from the goods and services produced in its commercial area, a sum to be divided by the amount of the currency, something regulated by the currency authority. By starting the UN$ as the US$ we start with a low-inflation currency riding on a particularly productive economy.

The Board of Governors of the IMF should compose an instruction to the IMF Executive Board to determine the least-change transformation from the US$ to the UN$, and then work on encouraging the preliminary steps in the US and the expansion of the International Reserve System first to other places where the US$ is already in use(e.g. Panama), then to places with currencies on par with the UN$(e.g. Argentina), then to those with a currency pegged to the UN$(e.g. Hong Kong), then elsewhere. The nonsense going on about a common European currency(for most of the fuss is indeed nonsense) could neatly be sidestepped.

The Governors' instruction should have some quite explicit details about the transformation of the U.S. Federal Reserve System into the UN International Reserve System, in case things get forgotten or fudged over in the Executive's transactions, to correct weaknesses in the FRS which we would prefer not to carry over.

The US has very little in the way of direct transfers, except for large amounts and on a regular basis. The IRB must from the start have the transfer capabilities to which, say, German bank clients are accustomed. The member banks(at least) would have to issue transfer as well as cheque forms to their customers.

The present US currency is physically unsuitable in some ways. Right from the beginning it should be clear that currency notes of different denominations should be of different size and color(all US ones are green). Also, similarly formatted coins should have greater denomination for greater weight. The 1¢, 2¢ and 5¢ coins should be of the same metal, probably the copper of the present-day "penny"; there is now no 2¢ piece, but there probably should be. Similarly, the dime, 2-dime and half-dollar coins should be of one metal; the quarter-dollar should probably be phased out to improve symmetry in the system. The $1, $2 and $5 coins should all be of the same format, either with edges(as the Susan B. Anthony dollar was meant to have) or of two metals, as some Italian coins are.

There would have to be at least 2 more digits in the bank sorting codes used by the FRB/IRB on cheques and comparable documents, both paper and electronic.

In addition, the instruction should have the Executive address certain specific problems of the application of an FRS-like IRS to the whole world.

The Federal Reserve System is not obligatory. There are U.S. banks for which its services are provided indirectly. This means that they have no reserve requirement, allowing money deposited with them to expand indefinitely(at least in principle, although that does not in fact happen even in the UK with the Thatcher-imposed zero reserve requirement). Germany has a finely tuned system of varying reserve rates for different kinds of deposit, but obviously if the IRB tried that even many member banks would be free enough of regulation to sidestep the reserve requirements. There is good argument that unit trusts should be subject to a reserve requirement: this might just be possible within the EuU, but not for a long time yet within the UN. The Executive will have to think hard about this, and will probably conclude that very fine manipulation of money supply can be foregone for the sake of common manipulation.

Federal Open Market operations are based on U.S. Government obligations. The ECB would have some messy co-ordination of operations in the obligations of all the member states but the IRB cannot be subject to such traded-off, Buggins-friendly directions in practice(it should not be, in theory, anyway). The amount of UN obligations, even including IBRD and IFC obligations, may be too small in proportion to the whole world's economy, and any preference for a particular state's obligations would constitute either unwarranted interference with or unfair favoritism for the bond market of that state.

Federal Open Market operations are performed on the New York Stock Exchange. By tradition there is no longer any complaint about this—I think there never was, because Wall Street was even more dominant within the U.S. in 1913 than it is now. Should the IRB operate on one exchange only, in days when we think of stock exchanges as rivals, or on a carve-up basis? After 20 years there might be no more dispute, but it is the first years we must think of.

Disputes about the FRB are settled in U.S. Federal courts. IRB disputes will probably need 2 levels of IMF court, with appeal possible to the ICJ, but it will not be that simple.

In Year 0, the regulatory functions of the FRB within the U.S. would have to be transferred to other agencies, e.g. the Comptroller of the Currency, the Federal Deposit Insurance Corporation. The administrative transformation would be quite hefty. It must be exactly specified, even though later rearrangement of the regulatory functions would be an internal U.S. affair.

Votes in the IMF and deposits at the IMF would be heavily modified in function(there is no need for inter-currency stabilization where there is only one currency). During the transition period the present function would continue, but at the end the IMF would probably find itself mainly an administrator of state and other crucial bankruptcies. The temptation to create money should be avoided by careful wording of the IRB Act. In the long run, the worldwide independent currency system should make for better fiscal behaviour, so there should be fewer such problems, but careful formulation is required for the early years.

FRB member banks are all investor- or customer-owned. Some IRB member banks would be state-owned. As much intra-district activity is decided by Bank rather than System boards, this may be significant: we do not want a wide-open discount window for badly run state banks to feed incompetent state-owned businesses. Also, the non-banker members of Bank boards(elected by the member banks) would often be subject to government direction if from state-owned firms. Such direction might be of just the kind an independent currency authority is supposed to sidestep and, in a world-wide system, would have funny-peculiar consequences comparable to those resulting from multiple currencies, though not so crude.

I think all these problems can be overcome, and that with a few weeks free run of a suitable library even I could work the rules out well enough, but someone does have to do it. How do I envisage things happening in the successive years of introduction of the IRB? Remember, the absorption of each currency authority in the IRB would depend on its currently sovereign supervising government relinquishing its rights.

Local Exchange Trading Systems would need no special help, each being able to work out its own new nexus with the general currency system(In Bath, for example, the prices in £ would become prices in UN$, but the prices in olivers would remain unchanged while the fees for LETS membership would, like all fees, have to be converted. Similar remarks apply to barter systems, although having a single currency may relieve the urge to barter for large enterprises. People partly isolated from the world's trading system should have no trouble adjusting to the new currency with which they access that trading system.

Except that the USA would have to be in from the beginning, there is no particular need to follow the list below slavishly, it is just the most sensible one I can think of. The entrance of each currently currency-sovereign "country" would be up to its government(s). It would have to be preceded by the stripping of regulatory functions from the currency authority and banks would probably have to close for a day or two to finish clearing transactions in the old currency. Also, the exact status of currency authority staff and buildings would have to be decided(the division of the world into IR Districts, each to have an IR Bank, would be decided before the expansion started), and due notice would have to be given to owners of slot machines. The old currency would become an IRB obligation at an agreed rate.

Year 0(possibly over several years).

The FRB, by purely internal U.S. statute, loses its regulatory functions, retaining its issue(including open-market), reserve and central-bank functions. The technical problems here are far less than obtaining the political will. The conversion of the FRB to the IRB might be decried as black helicopters stealing the U.S. currency. I also hazard a guess that the U.S. Constitution may supply some difficulty with the U.S. no longer being responsible for some erstwhile U.S. obligations(does the transfer constitute permission to question the credit of the U.S.?). I know this sounds a bit silly, but even sillier "constitutional" issues have been raised in the U.S. by apparently intelligent people, let alone raving nutters.

The said nutters might be horrified at the world "taking all our money away from us"(how many people recognize clearly that money has its value only from the goods and services upon which it gives call?). A few might be proud at the gift of this tremendous achievement to the world. A significant number might be pleased at the help the transfer of monetary authority

would give to the effort for a balanced budget, while the Left would oppose
the transfer precisely because of the desire for fiscal "flexibility".

With a single currency for the world, the U.S. tax system would be less
well able to keep tabs on dividend payments. But U.S. banking is so competent that comparatively few people would hold the bulk of their funds
abroad, and most of *them* are doing so already.

Many of these problems would arise as other currency blocs are
absorbed into the IRS, but the U.S. is the place where they have to be
tackled first, and also the place where their tackling makes the later work
minor in comparison.

Year 1.

January. The FRB becomes the IRB, by Acts of the IMF Board of
Governors and the U.S. Congress, the U.S. President being replaced in
Reserve Board functions by the IMF Executive Board and the U.S.
Congress in its such functions by the Board of Governors of the IMF. Any
necessary IMF courts open. The new currency starts getting
coined/printed at a replacement rate for the whole world, which is enough
to allow some initial stockpiling of specie, because there is no need for
immediate complete replacement of the US currency. The 13th IR Bank
opens in Panama/Panama and the 14th in Monrovia/Liberia, as Panama
and Liberia already use U.S. currency(those funny Liberian $5 notes can
be left as IOUs of the Liberian government).

February. Currencies with a one-one tie to the US$, and so now to the
UN$, become obligations of the International Reserve Board, IR Banks
being opened at suitable places in Argentina and the Bermuda Currency
Board closing. I think Argentina and Bermuda are the only countries in
this class. The Argentine currency authority has previously had any regulatory powers cut away, and at least some of its staff and buildings become
IRB staff and buildings. Like US$, the currencies of these territories are
freely exchangeable at IRB, but, again, there need be no hurry.

March. Currencies with a hard peg to the US$, now the UN$, notably the HK$, go the way of the Argentine currency, with the added difficulty of rapid exchange of specie being necessary.

April-December. Observe snags.

Year 2.

January. At a decided rate, the pound sterling becomes replaceable by the UN$, the B of E offices in the City, Manchester and Glasgow becoming IR Banks, the Birmingham office perhaps a branch of either London or Manchester, etc. As for HK, the currency must be fairly rapidly exchangeable.

February. As for Argentina with pound-par currencies(Malta only?).

March. As for HK, with hard-peg countries(Kenya?). Some countries maintaining a basket of reserve currencies will find themselves automatically with a hard peg, though perhaps not this early.

April-December. Observe snags.

Year 3.

January-March, as for pound in Year 2, against Japanese Yen.

April. Implement absorption agreements, where administratively possibly, with weak-peg currency authorities. The experience of the earlier years should now allow this extra task.

May-December. Observe snags.

Year 4.

As for Yen, with DM

Year 5.

As for Yen, with French Franc. Note particularly that the African Financial Community has a hard peg to the FF.

Year 6.

As for Yen, with PRC RMB Yuan. This may be very sticky, but getting a lot of people in the world currency system early helps prevent significant stubbornness later on.

Years 7—9.

As for Yen, with Russian Rubel, Indian Rupee and RSA Rand.

After the first few years the criteria of taking on might be varied, but the attempt should be to absorb territorial blocks; where this is difficult one currency important for its trade with the extant UN$ bloc, or for its internal wealth, or for its population, may be treated like the currencies of earlier years.

Once the IRB is functioning, international agencies should be encouraged to make the UN$ their currency of account. The UPU is the only UN agency not now using the US$(it uses gold francs), but regional organizations remain—we can get rid of the ecu years before the UN$ is the only currency in the EuU, and doing so would be helpful in many ways.

Once we have at least one functioning chamber of a directly elected UN Parliament(which we should not have before we have an effective court to monitor UN bodies' fidelity to basic human rights), it can assume the monetary functions of the IMF Board of governors. Once we have an elected UN Executive(which we should not have before we have a functioning bicameral Parliament), it can assume the monetary functions of the IMF Executive Board. Once we have general-jurisdiction UN courts, they can assume the functions here described for IMF courts.

1996.03.07

SELECTIVE PRISONS

Drako, great law-giver of Athens, was once asked why so many of the crimes in his calendar, crimes of very varying wickedness, attracted the death penalty. The lesser ones, he said, deserve that penalty, and there is nothing worse with which to punish the greater crimes. Anyone who has been tea-leafed can agree at least emotionally with Drako, but he was rather missing the point: one advantage of a state of government over a state of nature is that with government we no longer need to inflict the just penalty for each crime: lesser penalties are often more suitable, especially if the criminal knows that any greater crime than what he has already committed will attract a greater sentence. He must not think it as well to be hanged for a sheep as for a lamb, even so nasty a lamb as a well-fed thief.

There are a lot of things wrong with the criminal-justice system, starting with the delays in getting a criminal case before a magistrate. But what mostly seems to impinge on public consciousness is the prison subsystem, where we have the possibility of reforming the criminal(something Drako did not seem to consider) and so making for less crime in future, as well as for a more satisfactory life for those in economic and other intercourse with him. Still, Drako was right: when a prisoner is put in solitary for surrendering drugs and syringes to the prison staff(as happened recently), he quite probably deserves such punishment for his original crime. But wrong is being done in that he has committed no extra crime in helping the staff do a duty they do not want to do, and may even be showing signs of reform; and his good deed will no longer be a step towards full human decency: the Queen chooses, on appropriate advice, not to punish him so hard as he is now being punished.

Similarly, when prisoners have to sleep 8 to a small room with a bucket for a non-private privy, they may well deserve it: but the public at large do not deserve the repeated ill behaviour which may arise from such punishment, and God would much prefer the prison system to lead them towards a full human life—towards which in prison they can justly be compelled.

I am here assuming that all those in prison are guilty. That is not, of course the case. But my theme today is not the pre-conviction but the post-conviction procedure. I am interested in the post-crime life of the villain, and we know that the present system is far from optimal. But every proposal for improvement is subject to condemnations on ground of cost or softness, or, from another side, on grounds of cruelty. A partial answer may lie in the provision of specialist prisons for particular classes of criminal, perhaps sponsored as private prisons by those with bright ideas about prison reform—of whom, of course, I am one, albeit without funds to offer any service.

There already are specialized prisons. In England and Wales there are two prisons for mothers with young(under 2½ years) children, in which we try to punish the mother(mainly by restricting her liberty) without punishing the child(who has committed no crime). There is also a special prison, with bars on the bathroom walls, for geriatric lifers. I think we could use more.

Being a Catholic, I am interested in the Hierarchy of England and Wales sponsoring two differently selective prisons. Other kinds of selective prison should spring to mind as variations on these. Many Catholics vow themselves for life to various kinds of labour in service of the church, and societies of such may yield staff for some kinds of selective prison. There should be no over-crowding in selective prisons, because criminals for whom there is no room in the selective prisons can stay in the comprehensive ones, as at present: they have no right to enter a selective prison, and would not normally request it: no-one would have the right to remain in a comprehensive prison either.

In the two kinds of prison I am thinking of there would be no drug abuse. There is great drug abuse in today's prisons because the staff do not mind it: drugs keep the prisoners quiet. How this might be remedied in the comprehensives I do not here say, but in the selectives, each prisoner having his own room, and no prisoner needing much in the way of personal property, it should be possible to keep the place drug-free by excluding anyone on prescription drug use, whether by ingestion, inhalation or injection(perhaps tinactin for foot fungus can be allowed), searching all new arrivals thoroughly, putting most of their possessions in a lockbox till they leave, and monitoring their visits and mail thoroughly. No-one should have any current sickness not treatable by GP and no-one should have an addiction to meths(cold turkey can physiologically kill such addicts). This should not really cost much, and arriving junkies will by cold turkey lose their addiction soon enough(they are criminals, and in any case themselves chose to become addicted: they deserve the pain). Obviously, tobacco, alcohol, addictive and other mind-killing music, and most TV should be banned. We want to release free people, not slaves of any kind.

The first kind of selective prison would be a school, probably run by the Marists or the Christian Brothers, very much as they run schools in the wide world outside. The brothers chosen for this work should themselves be free of addiction and, of course, have healthy, natural eroticism(checkable by MMPI). The selection criteria would be:
1. age between 15 and 25 at entry(expulsion at 26);
2. at least one year of sentence to run, assuming all possible remission;
3. no more than 1 sexual invert in each of the 4 houses of the school;
4. baptized Catholic, not adherent of other church(certified by chaplain in remand or comprehensive prison);
5. no university degree or equivalent qualification.

This school should be remote from the criminals' usual haunts, and pretty near escape-proof—say on an islet off Barra with an office and waiting room in Castlebay. The islet should have a good supply of running water: cleanliness may be the first rung on the ladder to godliness, and these people have physiological as well as psychological and spiritual dirt to flush out. Teaching staff should reside permanently on the islet, guards coming in by boat from Castlebay.

The prisoner should be stripped of most of his possessions at the waiting room, being left with clothes and musical recordings(vetted), books(censored) and writing instruments. A second inspection should take place on arrival at the islet.

Each prisoner would have a small room to himself, with shelves sufficient for his books and some kind of music player, probably one for cassettes. The room should have built-in privy and washbasin, but showers and tubs would be elsewhere. There would be strict inspection to prevent vandalism.

Life for the prisoners would be thoroughly educational. Each would be assigned to a class, according not to age but to intellectual attainment. Each would be set a course of study, largely irrelevant of personal interest(although NEC or OU courses or other lines of clearly academic study already begun would usually be continued), and prepared for external exams. Every prisoner would be expected to work for at least 8 GCSEs followed by at least 5 Highers or AS Levels, followed by at least 2 A Levels followed by a degree, probably of the Open University(they would have to seek exemption from Summer School but the prison/school would try to make up for that).

Meals would be in a common refectory for each house, and would be compulsory. The food would be good, but not expensive, probably low on meat. There would be no alcohol available(the science teachers would be under an obligation to ensure that the equipment for making it was not available).

Daily mass would be available, and the teaching staff would participate, but it would not be compulsory. The chaplain would preferably be resident, and of another society than the teaching staff. A secular priest might be best. If no priest is available for residence, a curate from Barra should be asked to spend a lot of time at the prison.

There would be a television room in each house, and radio facilities, but only for use for explicit purposes, notably Open University for those studying. Perhaps the prisoners might watch the Queen's Christmas Message, but *not* the Cup Final. Nor would staff and, to keep them well-directed, there should be no television in *their* quarters either.

A library would get a good daily newspaper, so the prisoners could keep up with the world. How many of them would want to at first, with the usual media chosen by them at home cut off?

I envisage louts going in and being transformed to more conscious people free of addiction and oriented towards lifelong learning, even if with no *strong* urge towards it, and directed by hope for a better life, perhaps best sought in a new environment.

The other kind of selective prison would be a Carthusian monastery or a Camaldolese hermitage, run by some secular team but with, if volunteers can be found, a few suitable monks in residence for a few years each as examples for the prisoners. The selection criteria would be:

1. age over 35;
2. at least 10 years of sentence to run;
3. no more than one sexual invert;
4. baptized and confirmed Catholic, not adherent of other church(certified by chaplain in remand or comprehensive prison).

This prison would have 50 Carthusian-style cells(i.e. 4-room flats), each with a secluded garden. There would be common feeding, but the prisoners would be encouraged to make gardening part of their meditation and meditation their life till death. What we have in this prison will very often be people who will not leave alive, and orientation towards the afterlife is especially suitable for them. Silence could not be imposed, so any volunteer Carthusians or Camaldolese living with the prisoners would be making a great sacrifice—following a very gruelling call within the call to silence.

An ordinary(!) prison chaplain might be best for this prison, certainly not a monk. As always, residence is preferable but here particularly unlikely(one priest for 50 men... we have not the priests).

In both these prisons there would be a chance for quiet. The structure would orient the inmates to intelligence; the isolation from former haunts, even from former companions, would diminish much of the informational noise destructive of good orientation in life.

1996.06.06

New Jersey Adventure

NEW JERSEY ADVENTURE

There is in Stirling, on the borders of the Scottish Highlands and Lowlands, a firm hight IT-MacS, owned by the Begg-Lorimer family. The top person in the firm is Carole, and her main deputy is her husband, William, commonly called Bill. Their son Gavin runs their Stateside operations out of Athens in Georgia, often spending weeks at a time away from there to administer the arrival of new employees and their initial assignments. I understand that the firm gets some kind of subsidy from the Scottish Office.

IT-MacS hires IT professionals in Britain and rents them to U.S. firms, notably the Prudential Insurance Company in New Jersey, via an intermediary firm whose name I forget but whose principal hights Darrel. The contract is so arranged that the employees do not need U.S. residence rights and do not pay any income tax, either U.S. or home, because the salary gets paid partly as "expenses" and partly into an account in the Isle of Man. The firm provides apartments, one for two employees to share.

I saw an ad for IT-MacS in either *Computer Weekly* or the *Guardian*. The firm advertises mainly in the *Scotsman*. I telephoned for the application form, got it, filled it in, sent it in with a U.S.-oriented CV, and was very rapidly telephoned back by Bill. On 1996.07.10 I went for interview by Bill in Glasgow, when the firm's modus operandi was outlined to me. I pointed out that as a U.S. permanent resident I was legally obliged to file an income tax return every year, and had been doing so even during the five years when I was in the U.S. just enough not to lose my status. It was agreed that my salary, after deductions, would get paid into my U.S. bank account. There was a difficulty with my status at the time, and I showed Bill the special visa in my passport. He assured me that there would be no difficulty about it. I was left with the contract documents to read overnight(the firm had arranged a hotel room for me). The next morning we exchanged contracts on the understanding that I would fly to my new post in New Jersey on 1996.07.16, the following Tuesday.

Over that very busy weekend I was phoned several times by Carole, who was kept up to date on my packing arrangements(I was abandoning my digs in Stourbridge), in particular with my plan to send quite a bit by surface freight, despite which I would still probably have excess baggage. She also approved of my plan to spend Monday/Tuesday night with my brother in Lancing, not frightfully far from Gatwick.

On Monday I did travel to Lancing, making the horrendous discovery that Kings Cross Thameslink has no lifts, and on Tuesday by taxi to Gatwick, where, because of a sign I had made, I was found by the other two programmers in the shipment. When time came for check-in, problems did arise about my status. I telephoned Carole to discuss matters, and she telephoned around quite a lot. I was able to keep her informed also of a delay in the flight, and of the need for one of the other programmers to pay for the third's excess baggage. At length Carole discovered that the reason my Green Card(which would have obviated the need for the technique Bill thought suitable) had not arrived was something postal. I phoned my wife in Los Angeles to confirm a detail of that. Eventually the other programmers left on the flight to Newark, while I was directed by Carole to a lodging in Horsham. The next day, following instructions, I took the Gatwick Express to the U.S. Embassy and got a letter of transmission to make up for the missing Green Card. I spent one more night in Horsham and on 1996.07.18, Thursday, at Carole's instructions, assured that Gavin would be waiting for me at my destination airport, took the interairport bus to Heathrow and Air France. The latter had to get back to American Express, IT-MacS's travel agent, about my excess baggage.

Something went wrong with the Air France plane for Paris, so I was transferred, with many others, to a BA flight. Unfortunately, as I discovered once at Paris CDG, my baggage was not transferred, so it missed the flight to New York JFK. This was actually just as well, because Gavin was not there to meet me. After waving my sign around quite a lot, and having Gavin paged, I proceeded independently to Somerville. If I had been a little more awake, I might have remembered the new Subway line near the airport, built since my last visit to the Big Apple, but I used a more expensive route. I got to the apartment, to find things in reasonable order, and my flatmate in reasonably good humor despite my early-morning arrival. When morning came he told me that Gavin had been told I would be further delayed. When Gavin came, after my flatmate had gone to work(I was hanging around with a towel around me), he said he had expected me on a later flight but had nevertheless been at the airport at the time of my arrival. He professed not to understand how he could have missed my sign. He gave me preliminary instructions, mainly to wait for Darrel's phone call as to what to do on Monday. Gavin gives the impression of a sullen rotter, but, as is my wont, I charitably canceled this impression in my mind. A mistake. My luggage arrived on Friday/Saturday night.

On Sunday, just as I came back from church, Carole phoned and accused me of quarreling with Gavin, my flatmate, and Darrel. She threatened to fire me. The incident she mentioned with my flatmate was quite fictitious, and the others were too vague to respond to. She accused me of "attitude" for having the excess baggage. I managed to calm her down. I got the idea, which I still hold, that Gavin had taken a spite against me as a result of his failure to go to the airport, and was making trouble.

I worked Monday to Friday quite successfully at Prudential in Florham Park. I made visible progress on my assignment and my direct supervisor on Friday gave me instructions about Monday's work. During the week I spoke with Bill, who had gone to Athens, about my tax status. He was about to discuss it with the accountant in New York. Apparently I was the first employee, not excluding Gavin, to be U.S.-taxed.

On 1996.07.26, Friday, I handed my timesheet to Gary, the programmer entrusted with faxing them to Stirling. Later I met Gavin leaving my apartment and checked with him that he had been inside, because he had some mail there. He confirmed that he had been and told me that the Pru did not want me back on Monday because I had "been doing press-ups under someone's desk". He would see me about it later, either that evening or the next day. There was no discussion. I had indeed twice during the week remembered to do the physiotherapy prescribed for my bad back, but under a desk in a room where I was the only person working. I do not know who saw through the doorway and complained. I very much doubt that it was any of my immediate colleagues.

That night, instead of telling me my new assignment, Gavin got drunk(that is hearsay). The next day I stayed in so he could find me, but only got in touch with him because I sought him out at a neighbouring apartment when I heard he was there. He told me that I was not being reassigned, because of what I had done, especially after the other problems, which he did not specify(airport?). Again, there was no discussion.

On Sunday night, after I had started plans for new accommodation and a new job, Gavin phoned to say that I should be all ready packed because he and his father were coming at 08:30 the next morning to get me to the airport for a plane on Monday night. I said I had been thinking of looking for a job locally. He said that that was entirely up to me but that they needed the apartment.

At 1996.07.29—08:50, Bill and Gavin not having appeared, I left the apartment to visit the church, the newspapers, the Job Service, some potential employers and a lawyer. I left open on the kitchen table the state booklet about renting with ringed in red the paragraph about self-help evictions never being allowable in New Jersey, just in case they got any ideas. The lawyer, of the county legal services(not the county counsel), confirmed that they would have to give me two days written notice before seeking a court order, and that only after issue of a court order could my goods lawfully be removed from the apartment. At 15:20 I found the apartment stripped, at least of my possessions, and a note in the door with Gavin's telephone number. I went back to the lawyer, swore some affidavits, and heard him telephone Gavin and Bill, who got very annoyed with the lawyer's interpretation of the law(pretty obvious from the state booklet), and tried to insist that I should go to Scotland. It appeared that they had already surrendered their own lease on the apartment, presumably so that I would in case of reoccupation have to argue with the prime landlord rather than with them. The lawyer persuaded them to deliver my goods to the law office porch, which they with bad grace did(I later discovered that the list of people to be informed of my death was missing). I phoned the church for immediate aid in finding a place to stay overnight, although I had a legal right to go back to the apartment, because I did not want two balked thugs after me. The lawyer later said he could not blame me for not going back to the apartment, given Bill and Gavin's nastiness and "attitude".

At the time of writing I have not been paid my expenses(submitted to Gavin shortly after my arrival) or my salary for the week's work. Nor have I been compensated, as in principle I should be, for either the unjust dismissal or the illegal eviction.

1996.08.15

ABOUT THE AUTHOR

John A. Wills is a mathematician by education and an informatician by profession. He grew up in Kenya but has lived more in each of Europe and North American than in Africa. He currently lives in San Francisco, where he works in the City's Department of Public Health as a senior programmer and analyst. He is a parishioner of Saint Boniface in the Tenderloin. He has an eight-page Plan for himself on the inside of his front door. This book, part of the Plan, attempts to address problems he thinks central to his own life and the lives of others. He used to be a member of the German Liberal party but is no longer certain that he is a liberal; he knows he is not a pseudoliberal of current fashion.

www.ingramcontent.com/pod-product-compliance
Lightning Source LLC
Chambersburg PA
CBHW021604280526
45784CB00001BA/499